MW01609610

DONATED IN MEMORY OF

ROBERT PELTON

SHAKESPEARE

JULIUS
CAESAR

REVIEW
QUESTIONS & ANSWERS

COLES EDITORIAL BOARD

OTABIND

ABOUT ░░░░ NOTES

░░░░ NOTES have been an indispensible aid to students on five continents since 1948.

░░░░ NOTES are available for a wide range of individual literary works. Clear, concise explanations and insights are provided along with interesting interpretations and evaluations.

Proper use of ░░░░ NOTES will allow the student to pay greater attention to lectures and spend less time taking notes. This will result in a broader understanding of the work being studied and will free the student for increased participation in discussions.

░░░░ NOTES are an invaluable aid for review and exam preparation as well as an invitation to explore different interpretive paths.

░░░░ NOTES are written by experts in their fields. It should be noted that any literary judgement expressed herein is just that – the judgement of one school of thought. Interpretations that diverge from, or totally disagree with any criticism may be equally valid.

░░░░ NOTES are designed to supplement the text and are not intended as a substitute for reading the text itself. Use of the NOTES will serve not only to clarify the work being studied, but should enhance the readers enjoyment of the topic.

ISBN 0-7740-2934-X

© COPYRIGHT 1998 AND PUBLISHED BY
COLES PUBLISHING COMPANY
TORONTO - CANADA
PRINTED IN CANADA

Manufactured by Webcom Limited
Cover finish: Webcom's Exclusive DURACOAT

CONTENTS

Page No.

Part A: The Play in Brief

Introduction

As enjoyable and important as Shakespeare's plays are, they can be difficult to read. Since Shakespeare wrote his plays to appeal to Elizabethan audiences, much of the text is dated and means little to the average reader of today.

We are, therefore, presenting the substance of the play in readable form by eliminating, as much as possible, the outdated passages and by paraphrasing the more complicated ones. This will give you a better understanding and appreciation of the play, and will make the questions and answers more meaningful.

CHARACTERS IN THE PLAY

Julius Caesar

Octavius Caesar
Marcus Antonius (also **Mark** or **Marc Antony**) — Triumvirs after the death of Julius Caesar.
M. Aemilius Lepidus

Cicero
Publius — Senators.
Popilius Lena

Marcus Brutus
Cassius
Casca
Trebonius — Conspirators against Julius Caesar.
Ligarius
Decius Brutus
Metellus Cimber

Cinna
Flavius — Tribunes.
Marullus

Artemidorus: A teacher of rhetoric.
Soothsayer
Cinna: A poet.
Another Poet

Lucilius
Titinius
Messala — Friends of Brutus and Cassius.
Young Cato
Volumnius

Varro
Clitus
Claudius } Brutus' servants.
Strato
Lucius
Dardanius
Pindarus: Cassius' servant.
Calphurnia: Caesar's wife.
Portia: Brutus' wife.
Senators, Citizens, Guards and Attendants
[*Setting: Rome, Sardis and near Philippi.*]

ACT I

The Roman citizens are gathering in the streets to celebrate Caesar's triumphant return to the city after his successful war against Pompey. Two tribunes, Flavius and Marullus, enter and order the citizens to leave the streets. These tribunes, who are supposed to protect the rights of the common people, are in league with the republican aristocrats, who have been bitterly criticizing Caesar and who are now plotting his murder.

Although the citizens are not pleased about having their celebration cut short, they obey the tribunes and leave, after making their dissatisfaction known. Flavius and Marullus then remove the decorations from the statues of Caesar and his ancestors.

A general shout and a flourish of trumpets announce the approach of Caesar, followed by a large crowd. The procession is heading for the Forum to celebrate the Feast of the Lupercal, during which the younger public officials, stripped to the waist, participate in a foot race. Caesar remarks to Antony, one of the runners:

> Forget not in your speed, Antonius,
> To touch Calphurnia; for our elders say
> The barren, touchèd in this holy chase,
> Shake off this sterile curse.

From the crowd, a soothsayer calls to Caesar to "Beware the ides of March" (March 15), but Caesar dismisses him scornfully as a dreamer.

While the others walk ahead, Cassius and Brutus remain to discuss the possibility that Caesar will be offered the crown. Cassius tries to learn Brutus' attitude toward Caesar. Cassius reveals his own burning resentment for Caesar and he leads Brutus to confess that, although he is fond of Caesar personally, he does not approve of Caesar's assuming royal power. Cassius then proceeds to flatter Brutus:

> I know that virtue to be in you, Brutus,
> As well as I do know your outward favour.
> Well, honour is the subject of my story.
> I cannot tell what you and other men
> Think of this life, but, for my single self,

I had as lief not be as live to be
In awe of such a thing as I myself.

Cassius also reveals his contempt for Caesar:

He had a fever when he was in Spain,
And when the fit was on him, I did mark
How he did shake: 'tis true, this god did shake;
His coward lips did from their colour fly,
And that same eye whose bend doth awe the world
Did lose his lustre: I did hear him groan:
Ay, and that tongue of his that bade the Romans
Mark him and write his speeches in their books,
Alas, it cried, 'Give me some drink, Titinius,'
As a sick girl. Ye gods! it doth amaze me
A man of such a feeble temper should
So get the start of the majestic world
And bear the palm alone.

Hearing a general shout from the Forum, Brutus guesses that "these applauses are/For some new honours that are heap'd on Caesar." Cassius angrily breaks out:

Why, man, he doth bestride the narrow world
Like a Colossus, and we petty men
Walk under his huge legs and peep about
To find ourselves dishonourable graves.
Men at some time are masters of their fates:
The fault, dear Brutus, is not in our stars,
But in ourselves, that we are underlings.
Brutus, and Caesar: what should be in that Caesar?
Why should that name be sounded more than yours?
Write them together, yours is as fair a name;
Sound them, it doth become the mouth as well;
Weigh them, it is as heavy; conjure with 'em,
Brutus will start a spirit as soon as Caesar.
Now, in the names of all the gods at once,
Upon what meat doth this our Caesar feed,
That he is grown so great? Age, thou art shamed!
Rome, thou hast lost the breed of noble bloods!
When went there by an age, since the great flood,
But it was famed with more than with one man?

When could they say till now that talk'd of Rome
That her wide walls encompass'd but one man?
Now is it Rome indeed, and room enough,
When there is in it but one only man.
O, you and I have heard our fathers say
There was a Brutus once that would have brook'd
The eternal devil to keep his state in Rome
As easily as a king.

Brutus promises to consider Cassius' views, and Cassius is pleased that his "weak words have struck but thus much show/Of fire from Brutus."

Now they hear the noise of the returning crowd, and Caesar appears with what Brutus calls the glow of anger on his cheeks. When he sees Cassius, Caesar turns to Antony and says:

Let me have men about me that are fat,
Sleek-headed men, and such as sleep o' nights:
Yond Cassius has a lean and hungry look;
He thinks too much: such men are dangerous.
Antony: Fear him not, Caesar; he's not dangerous;
He is a noble Roman, and well given.
Caesar: Would he were fatter! but I fear him not:
Yet if my name were liable to fear,
I do not know the man I should avoid
So soon as that spare Cassius. He reads much;
He is a great observer, and he looks
Quite through the deeds of men: he loves no plays,
As thou dost, Antony; he hears no music:
Seldom he smiles, and smiles in such a sort
As if he mock'd himself, and scorn'd his spirit
That could be moved to smile at any thing.
Such men as he be never at heart's ease
Whiles they behold a greater than themselves,
And therefore are they very dangerous.
I rather tell thee what is to be fear'd
Than what I fear; for always I am Caesar.
'Come on my right hand, for this ear is deaf,
And tell me truly what thou think'st of him.

As Caesar leaves, Brutus and Cassius detain Casca, who has been at the Forum, and ask him what happened there.

Casca replies that, each time Caesar was offered the crown by Antony and refused it, there was a shout of encouragement from the crowd. When Brutus asks for a more complete description of what happened, Casca says:

> I can as well be hang'd as tell the manner of it: it was mere foolery; I did not mark it. I saw Mark Antony offer him a crown: yet 'twas not a crown neither, 'twas one of these coronets: and, as I told you, he put it by once: but for all that, to my thinking, he would fain have had it. Then he offered it to him again; then he put it by again: but, to my thinking, he was very loath to lay his fingers off it. And then he offered it the third time; he put it the third time by: and still as he refused it, the rabblement hooted and clapped their chopped hands and threw up their sweaty night-caps and uttered such a deal of stinking breath because Caesar refused the crown, that it had almost choked Caesar; for he swounded and fell down at it: and for mine own part, I durst not laugh, for fear of opening my lips and receiving the bad air.

Thus, we learn that Caesar also had an epileptic fit. When he came to himself, he apologized for anything he may have said during the fit and he left, greatly upset. At the conclusion of Casca's story, Brutus leaves, inviting Cassius to continue their discussion later at his house. Cassius is left alone with his thoughts:

> Well, Brutus, thou art noble; yet, I see,
> Thy honourable metal may be wrought
> From that it is disposed: therefore it is meet
> That noble minds keep ever with their likes;
> For who so firm that cannot be seduced?
> Caesar doth bear me hard; but he loves Brutus:
> If I were Brutus now and he were Cassius,
> He should not humour me. I will this night,
> In several hands, in at his windows throw,
> As if they came from several citizens,
> Writings, all tending to the great opinion
> That Rome holds of his name, wherein obscurely
> Caesar's ambition shall be glanced at:

And after this let Caesar seat him sure;
For we will shake him, or worse days endure.

It is now night. There is a violent storm raging, with thunder and lightning. In the midst of it, Casca and Cicero meet. Casca is greatly disturbed by the storm and the omens accompanying it. He says to Cicero:

A common slave—you know him well by sight—
Held up his left hand, which did flame and burn
Like twenty torches join'd, and yet his hand
Not sensible of fire remain'd unscorch'd.
Besides—I ha' not since put up my sword
Against the Capitol I met a lion,
Who glared upon me and went surly by
Without annoying me: and there were drawn
Upon a heap a hundred ghastly women
Transformed with their fear, who swore they saw
Men all in fire walk up and down the streets.
And yesterday the bird of night did sit
Even at noon-day upon the market-place,
Hooting and shrieking. When these prodigies
Do so conjointly meet, let not men say
'These are their reasons: they are natural;'
For, I believe, they are portentous things
Unto the climate that they point upon.

Cicero, who is not as easily frightened as Casca, asks whether Caesar is going to the Capitol in the morning. When Casca says he is, Cicero says good night and returns to his home, saying "This disturbèd sky/Is not to walk in."

Cassius now enters and begins to boast about his fearlessness:

For my part, I have walked about the streets,
Submitting me unto the perilous night,
And, thus unbracèd, Casca, as you see,
Have bared my bosom to the thunder-stone;
And when the cross blue lightning seemed to open
The breast of heaven, I did present myself
Even in the aim and very flash of it.

7

Casca is surprised at such daring, but to Cassius, these "strange eruptions" are nothing more than omens of "fear and warning unto some monstrous evil." Thus, he brings the talk around to Caesar. Tomorrow, says Casca, the senators are "to establish Caesar as a king." This, Cassius says, will be the signal for him to take his own life: "Cassius from bondage will deliver Cassius." Hearing this, Casca joins the ranks of the conspirators. Then Cinna enters and is given various papers by Cassius, who directs him:

Be you content: good Cinna, take this paper,
And look you lay it in the praetor's chair,
Where Brutus may but find it, and throw this
In at his window; set this up with wax
Upon old Brutus' statue: all this done,
Repair to Pompey's porch, where you shall find us.

Cassius then turns to Casca:

Come, Casca, you and I will yet ere day
See Brutus at his house: three parts of him
Is ours already, and the man entire
Upon the next encounter yields him ours.
Casca: O, he sits high in all the people's hearts;
And that which would appear offence in us
His countenance, like richest alchemy,
Will change to virtue and to worthiness.
Cassius: Him and his worth and our great need of him
You have right well conceited. Let us go,
For it is after midnight, and ere day
We will awake him and be sure of him.

ACT II

During the night, Brutus finds himself unable to sleep. He calls his servant, Lucius, to light a candle in the study. Lucius returns and hands Brutus an anonymous letter. This letter, like the ones Brutus has found before, is actually from Cassius and it urges Brutus to take action against Caesar.

After reading the letter, Brutus reviews his reasons for joining the conspiracy to murder Caesar:

It must be by his death: and, for my part,
I know no personal cause to spurn at him,
But for the general. He would be crown'd:
How that might change his nature, there's the question:
It is the bright day that brings forth the adder;
And that craves wary walking. Crown him? That.
And then, I grant, we put a sting in him,
That at his will he may do danger with.
The abuse of greatness is when it disjoins
Remorse from power: and, to speak truth of Caesar,
I have not known when his affections sway'd
More than his reason. But 'tis a common proof,
That lowliness is young ambition's ladder,
Whereto the climber-upward turns his face;
But when he once attains the upmost round,
He then unto the ladder turns his back,
Looks in the clouds, scorning the base degrees
By which he did ascend: so Caesar may;
Then, lest he may, prevent. And, since the quarrel
Will bear no colour for the thing he is,
Fashion it thus; that what he is, augmented,
Would run to these and these extremities:
And therefore think him as a serpent's egg
Which hatch'd would as his kind grow mischievous,
And kill him in the shell.

Lucious enters to announce the arrival of Cassius and five others. Brutus sends Lucius to let the men in. When the boy is gone, Brutus says to himself:

They are the faction. O conspiracy,
Shamest thou to show thy dangerous brow by night,
When evils are most free? O, then, by day
Where wilt thou find a cavern dark enough
To mask thy monstrous visage? Seek none,
conspiracy;
Hide it in smiles and affability:
For if thou path, thy native semblance on,
Not Erebus itself were dim enough
To hide thee from prevention.

The conspirators enter, and Brutus welcomes each one.
Cassius suggests that they take a mutual oath of faithfulness,
but Brutus objects:

No, not an oath: if not the face of men,
The sufferance of our souls, the time's abuse,
If these be motives weak, break off betimes,
And every man hence to his idle bed;
So let high-sighted tyranny range on
Till each man drop by lottery. . . .
Swear priests and cowards and men cautelous,
Old feeble carrions and such suffering souls
That welcome wrongs; unto bad causes swear
Such creatures as men doubt: but do not stain
The even virtue of our enterprise,
Nor the insuppressive mettle of our spirits,
To think that or our cause or our performance
Did need an oath; when every drop of blood
That every Roman bears, and nobly bears,
Is guilty of a several bastardy
If he do break the smallest particle
Of any promise that hath pass'd from him.

Then they consider whether Antony should be killed along
with Caesar, as Cassius wishes. Brutus disagrees again:

Our course will seem too bloody, Caius Cassius,
To cut the head off and then hack the limbs,
Like wrath in death and envy afterwards;
For Antony is but a limb of Caesar:
Let us be sacrificers, but not butchers, Caius.

We all stand up against the spirit of Caesar,
And in the spirit of men there is no blood:
O, that we then could come by Caesar's spirit,
And not dismember Caesar! But, alas,
Caesar must bleed for it! And, gentle friends,
Let's kill him boldly, but not wrathfully;
Let's carve him as a dish fit for the gods,
Not hew him as a carcass fit for hounds:
And let our hearts, as subtle masters do,
Stir up their servants to an act of rage
And after seem to chide 'em. This shall make
Our purpose necessary and not envious:
Which so appearing to the common eyes,
We shall be call'd purgers, not murderers.
And for Mark Antony, think not of him;
For he can do no more than Caesar's arm
When Caesar's head is off.
Cassius: Yet I fear him,
For in the ingrafted love he bears to Caesar—
Brutus: Alas, good Cassius, do not think of him:
If he love Caesar, all that he can do
Is to himself, take thought and die for Caesar:
And that were much he should, for he is given
To sports, to wildness and much company.
Trebonius: There is no fear in him; let him not die;
For he will live and laugh at this hereafter.

One of the conspirators wonders whether the strange events of this wild night will stop Caesar from going to the Capitol. But Decius Brutus says he can talk Caesar out of any superstitious fears he may have:

Never fear that: if he be so resolved,
I can o'ersway him; for he loves to hear
That unicorns may be betray'd with trees
And bears with glasses, elephants with holes,
Lions with toils and men with flatterers:
But when I tell him he hates flatterers,
He says he does, being then most flattered.
Let me work;
For I can give his humour the true bent,
And I will bring him to the Capitol.

All of them agree to meet at eight in the morning to escort Caesar to the Capitol. It is now early dawn. As they separate, Brutus tells them to behave "fresh and merrily" and adds, "Let not our looks put on our purposes."

Then he turns to the sleeping Lucius:

Boy! Lucius! Fast asleep! It is no matter;
Enjoy the honey-heavy dew of slumber:
Thou hast no figures nor no fantasies,
Which busy care draws in the brains of men;
Therefore thou sleep'st so sound.

Portia, concerned about Brutus, enters and speaks to him:

You've ungently, Brutus,
Stole from my bed: and yesternight at supper
You suddenly arose and walk'd about,
Musing and sighing, with your arms across;
And when I ask'd you what the matter was,
You stared upon me with ungentle looks:
I urged you further; then you scratch'd your head,
And too impatiently stamp'd with your foot:
Yet I insisted, yet you answer'd not,
But with an angry wafture of your hand
Gave sign for me to leave you: so I did,
Fearing to strengthen that impatience
Which seem'd too much enkindled, and withal
Hoping it was but an effect of humour,
Which sometime hath his hour with every man.
It will not let you eat, nor talk, nor sleep,
And, could it work so much upon your shape
As it hath much prevail'd on your condition,
I should not know you, Brutus. Dear my lord,
Make me acquainted with your cause of grief.

Brutus assures his wife that he is simply not feeling well, but Portia doubts that his troubles are only physical:

Is Brutus sick, and is it physical
To walk unbraced and suck up the humours
Of the dank morning? What, is Brutus sick,
And will he steal out of his wholesome bed,

To dare the vile contagion of the night,
And tempt the rheumy and unpurged air
To add unto his sickness? No, my Brutus;
You have some sick offence within your mind,
Which by the right and virtue of my place
I ought to know of: and, upon my knees,
I charm you, by my once commended beauty,
By all your vows of love and that great vow
Which did incorporate and make us one,
That you unfold to me, yourself, your half,
Why you are heavy, and what men to-night
Have had resort to you; for here have been
Some six or seven, who did hide their faces
Even from darkness.

Portia goes on to accuse Brutus of not loving her because he does not share his secrets with her:

Dwell I but in the suburbs
Of your good pleasure? If it be no more,
Portia is Brutus' harlot, not his wife.

Portia reminds Brutus of how she has proved herself a noble and courageous wife:

I grant I am a woman, but withal
A woman that Lord Brutus took to wife:
I grant I am a woman, but withal
A woman well reputed, Cato's daughter.
Think you I am no stronger than my sex,
Being so father'd and so husbanded?
Tell me your counsels, I will not disclose 'em:
I have made strong proof of my constancy,
Giving myself a voluntary wound
Here in the thigh: can I bear that with patience
And not my husband's secrets?

Brutus is so moved by Portia's speech that he asks the gods to make him worthy of this noble wife. Then he promises Portia he will soon reveal to her "all the charactery of my sad brows."

Lucius enters with Caius Ligarius, whom Brutus persuades to join the conspirators.

The thunder and lightning continue as Caesar, in his dressing gown, appears in his home. Calphurnia has had dreams foreboding his murder, so he has arisen early to send a servant to have the priests offer sacrifices and to bring him "their opinion of success." Calphurnia now comes into the room and insists that the omens of the night have frightened her. Caesar, she is determined, must not go out this day:

> When beggars die, there are no comets seen;
> The heavens themselves blaze forth the death of
> princes.
> **Caesar:** Cowards die many times before their deaths;
> The valiant never taste of death but once.
> Of all the wonders that I yet have heard,
> It seems to me most strange that men should fear;
> Seeing that death, a necessary end,
> Will come when it will come.

At this moment, the servant returns to report that the sacrifices are not favorable, but Caesar remains intent upon going out:

> The gods do this in shame of cowardice:
> Caesar should be a beast without a heart
> If he should stay at home to-day for fear.
> No, Caesar shall not: danger knows full well
> That Caesar is more dangerous than he:
> We are two lions litter'd in one day,
> And I the elder and more terrible:
> And Caesar shall go forth.

Calphurnia still insists that Caesar remain home, and, finally, it is decided that Caesar will stay in, not through his fear, but Calphurnia's. When Decius Brutus comes to accompany Caesar to the senate house and Caesar says he will not go out, Decius wants to know the reason. Caesar confesses that Calphurnia keeps him at home:

> She dreamt to-night she saw my statua,
> Which like a fountain with an hundred spouts
> Did run pure blood, and many lusty Romans
> Came smiling and did bathe their hands in it:

And these does she apply for warnings and portents
And evils imminent, and on her knee
Hath begg'd that I will stay at home to-day.

Decius interprets this dream in a highly favorable light:

This dream is all amiss interpreted;
It was a vision fair and fortunate:
Your statue spouting blood in many pipes,
In which so many smiling Romans bathed,
Signifies that from you great Rome shall suck
Reviving blood, and that great men shall press
For tinctures, stains, relics and cognizance.
This by Calphurnia's dream is signified.

Upon hearing this interpretation of the dream, Caesar decides to go, especially as Decius tells him the senate has set this day to give him a crown—it would be unfortunate to postpone such an event.

While Decius is talking with Caesar, the group of conspirators enters, followed by Antony, to conduct him to the Capitol.

Meanwhile, Artemidorus takes his stand on the street down which Caesar must pass, intending to hand him a letter that exposes the whole conspiracy.

Portia, who is now obviously aware of the plot to murder Caesar, appears on the street in a state of great excitement. She orders Lucius to bring her news from the Capitol. Then, the soothsayer enters, and she asks him for news. When the soothsayer indicates that he may know about the conspiracy and is going to warn Caesar, Portia is alarmed. But she is relieved to learn that the soothsayer only fears a plot, without knowing of one. Feeling faint, she starts to return home, saying:

I must go in. Ay me, how weak a thing
The heart of woman is! O Brutus,
The heavens speed thee in thine enterprise!
Sure, the boy heard me. Brutus hath a suit
That Caesar will not grant. O, I grow faint.
Run, Lucius, and commend me to my lord;
Say I am merry: come to me again,
And bring me word what he doth say to thee.

ACT III

Artemidorus and the soothsayer stand among the crowd gathered in front of the Capitol. Caesar arrives, surrounded by the conspirators. Caesar remarks to the soothsayer, "The ides of March are come." The soothsayer replies, "Ay, Caesar, but not gone." Artemidorus presents his letter, saying that it concerns Caesar personally. For this very reason, Caesar puts it aside to be considered later and enters the senate house. Trebonius draws Mark Antony away, and then the conspirators crowd around Caesar in support of a petition presented by Metellus Cimber. On his knees, Cimber asks Caesar to call back from punishment his brother, Publius Cimber. Brutus and Cassius support his plea, but Caesar turns to them and says:

> I could be well moved, if I were as you;
> If I could pray to move, prayers would move me:
> But I am constant as the northern star,
> Of whose true-fix'd and resting quality
> There is no fellow in the firmament.
> The skies are painted with unnumber'd sparks;
> They are all fire and every one doth shine;
> But there's but one in all doth hold his place:
> So in the world; 'tis furnish'd well with men,
> And men are flesh and blood, and apprehensive;
> Yet in the number I do know but one
> That unassailable holds on his rank,
> Unshaked of motion: and that I am he,
> Let me a little show it, even in this;
> That I was constant Cimber should be banish'd.
> And constant do remain to keep him so.

Then Casca, in apparent panic, attempts to plunge his dagger into the back of Caesar's neck. Casca strikes a clumsy blow, but the others move in and repeatedly stab Caesar, who stops resisting when he sees Brutus among them.

As Caesar dies, chaos breaks out. Brutus and Cassius are attempting to control the general panic when Trebonius returns and reports that Antony has fled to his house, "amazed." He goes on to say:

Men, wives and children stare, cry out and run
As it were doomsday.

Cassius and Brutus now attempt to justify the death of
Caesar:

Cassius: Why, he that cuts off twenty years of life
Cuts off so many years of fearing death.
Brutus: Grant that, and then is death a benefit:
So are we Caesar's friends, that have abridged
His time of fearing death. Stoop, Romans, stoop,
And let us bathe our hands in Caesar's blood
Up to the elbows, and besmear our swords:
Then walk we forth, even to the market-place,
And waving our red weapons o'er our heads,
Let's all cry 'Peace, freedom and liberty!'
Cassius: Stoop then, and wash. How many ages
hence
Shall this our lofty scene be acted over
In states unborn and accents yet unknown!
Brutus: How many times shall Caesar bleed in sport,
That now on Pompey's basis lies along
No worthier than the dust!
Cassius: So oft as that shall be,
So often shall the knot of us be call'd
The men that gave their country liberty.

Antony's servant comes in and, kneeling, speaks to Brutus:

Thus, Brutus, did my master bid me kneel;
Thus did Mark Antony bid me fall down;
And, being prostrate, thus he bade me say:
Brutus is noble, wise, valiant and honest;
Caesar was mighty, bold, royal and loving:
Say I love Brutus and I honour him;
Say I fear'd Caesar, honour'd him and loved him.
If Brutus will vouchsafe that Antony
May safely come to him and be resolved
How Caesar hath deserved to lie in death,
Mark Antony shall not love Caesar dead
So well as Brutus living, but will follow
The fortunes and affairs of noble Brutus

Thorough the hazards of this untrod state
With all true faith. So says my master Antony.

Brutus instructs the servant to have Antony come to them. He promises that Antony will not be harmed. He assures the others that Antony will join them as a friend. Cassius still has doubts about Antony's loyalties, though.

Antony enters and, making no attempt to hide his grief, addresses Caesar's body and advises the conspirators to kill him now too, if that is their intention:

O mighty Caesar! dost thou lie so low?
Are all thy conquests, glories, triumphs, spoils,
Shrunk to this little measure? Fare thee well.
I know not, gentlemen, what you intend,
Who else must be let blood, who else is rank:
If I myself, there is no hour so fit
As Caesar's death's hour, nor no instrument
Of half that worth as those your swords, made rich
With the most noble blood of all this world.
I do beseech ye, if you bear me hard,
Now, whilst your purpled hands do reek and smoke,
Fulfil your pleasure. Live a thousand years,
I shall not find myself so apt to die:
No place will please me so, no mean of death,
As here by Caesar, and by you cut off,
The choice and master spirits of this age.

But Brutus assures Antony:

O Antony, beg not your death of us.
Though now we must appear bloody and cruel,
As, by our hands and this our present act
You see we do; yet see you but our hands
And this the bleeding business they have done:
Our hearts you see not; they are pitiful;
And pity to the general wrong of Rome
As fire drives out fire, so pity pity
Hath done this deed on Caesar. For your part,
To you our swords have leaden points, Mark
Antony:
Our arms in strength of malice, and our hearts

Of brothers' temper, do receive you in
With all kind love, good thoughts and reverence.

Brutus promises Antony a full explanation later, when the people have been calmed. Antony shakes the conspirators' hands in a pledge of friendship and proceeds to explain his delicate position:

Gentlemen all—alas, what shall I say?
My credit now stands on such slippery ground,
That one of two bad ways you must conceit me,
Either a coward or a flatterer.
That I did love thee, Caesar, O, 'tis true:
If then thy spirit look upon us now,
Shall it not grieve thee dearer than thy death,
To see thy Antony making his peace,
Shaking the bloody fingers of thy foes,
Most noble! in the presence of thy corse?
Had I as many eyes as thou hast wounds,
Weeping as fast as they stream forth thy blood,
It would become me better than to close
In terms of friendship with thine enemies.
Pardon me, Julius! Here wast thou bay'd, brave hart;
Here didst thou fall, and here thy hunters stand,
Sign'd in thy spoil and crimson'd in thy lethe.
O world, thou wast the forest to this hart;
And this, indeed, O world, the heart of thee.
How like a deer strucken by many princes
Dost thou here lie!

Cassius is anxious to know what arrangements Antony wishes to make with them. He replies that he wishes to be friends, provided they will show him why Caesar was dangerous. Beyond that, all he wishes is the privilege of speaking at Caesar's funeral. Brutus consents. Again, Cassius objects, and, again, Brutus overrules his objections by saying that he will speak first, showing the reasons for Caesar's death and telling the people that, with Brutus' consent, Antony will speak over Caesar's body.

Leaving the body with Antony, Brutus and the others go out. Antony expresses his true feelings in a soliloquy:

O, pardon me, thou bleeding piece of earth,
That I am meek and gentle with these butchers!
Thou art the ruins of the noblest man
That ever lived in the tide of times.
Woe to the hand that shed this costly blood!
Over thy wounds now do I prophesy,
Which like dumb mouths do ope their ruby lips
To beg the voice and utterance of my tongue,
A curse shall light upon the limbs of men;
Domestic fury and fierce civil strife
Shall cumber all the parts of Italy;
Blood and destruction shall be so in use,
And dreadful objects so familiar,
That mothers shall but smile when they behold
Their infants quarter'd with the hands of war;
All pity choked with custom of fell deeds:
And Caesar's spirit ranging for revenge,
With Ate by his side come hot from hell,
Shall in these confines with a monarch's voice
Cry 'Havoc,' and let slip the dogs of war;
That this foul deed shall smell above the earth
With carrion men, groaning for burial.

A servant from Octavius comes to Antony. Seeing the body of Caesar, he is shocked. Both he and Antony begin to weep, and Antony tells him to wait until after the funeral speech before returning to Octavius to tell him the people's reaction.

Brutus and Cassius, with a crowd of citizens, now enter the Forum. The citizens are demanding to know the reason for Caesar's murder. Some of the people go with Cassius to hear his explanation, but the rest surround Brutus as he addresses them:

Be patient till the last.
Romans, countrymen, and lovers! hear me for my cause, and be silent, that you may hear: believe me for mine honour, and have respect to mine honour, that you may believe: censure me in your wisdom, and awake your senses, that you may the better judge. If there be any in this assembly, any dear friend of Caesar's, to him I say that Brutus' love to Caesar was no less than his. If then that friend demand why Brutus rose against Caesar, this is my answer: not that

I loved Caesar less, but that I loved Rome more. Had you rather Caesar were living, and die all slaves, than that Caesar were dead, to live all freemen? As Caesar loved me, I weep for him; as he was fortunate, I rejoice at it; as he was valiant, I honour him; but as he was ambitious, I slew him. There is tears for his love; joy for his fortune; honour for his valour; and death for his ambition. Who is here so base that would be a bondman? If any, speak; for him have I offended. Who is here so rude that would not be a Roman? If any, speak; for him have I offended. Who is here so vile that will not love his country? If any, speak; for him have I offended. I pause for a reply.

Hearing no reply, Brutus concludes, "Then none have I offended."

Now Antony enters with Caesar's body. Brutus steps down, saying:

With this I depart—that, as I slew my best lover for the good of Rome, I have the same dagger for myself, when it shall please my country to need my death.

His speech is received favorably by the citizens, who wish to "bring him with triumph home unto his house." But Brutus asks them, for his sake, to stay and listen to Antony. They consent, although they are quite persuaded that Caesar's death was justified.

Antony goes up to the platform where Brutus had just spoken and begins his speech:

Friends, Romans, countrymen, lend me your ears;
I come to bury Caesar, not to praise him.
The evil that men do lives after them;
The good is oft interred with their bones;
So let it be with Caesar. The noble Brutus
Hath told you Caesar was ambitious:
If it were so, it was a grievous fault,
And grievously hath Caesar answer'd it.
Here, under leave of Brutus and the rest,
For Brutus is an honourable man;
So are they all, all honourable men,

Come I to speak in Caesar's funeral.
He was my friend, faithful and just to me:
But Brutus says he was ambitious;
And Brutus is an honourable man.
He hath brought many captives home to Rome,
Whose ransoms did the general coffers fill:
Did this in Caesar seem ambitious?
When that the poor have cried, Caesar hath wept:
Ambition should be made of sterner stuff:
Yet Brutus says he was ambitious;
And Brutus is an honourable man.
You all did see that on the Lupercal
I thrice presented him a kingly crown,
Which he did thrice refuse: was this ambition?
Yet Brutus says he was ambitious;
And, sure, he is an honourable man.
I speak not to disprove what Brutus spoke,
But here I am to speak what I do know.
You all did love him once, not without cause:
What cause withholds you then to mourn for him?
O judgement! thou art fled to brutish beasts,
And men have lost their reason. Bear with me;
My heart is in the coffin there with Caesar,
And I must pause till it come back to me.

During this pause, the citizens comment among themselves.
They agree that there is much reason in what Antony says and
note how deeply he is himself affected: "his eyes are red with
weeping." Then Antony continues:

But yesterday the word of Caesar might
Have stood against the world: now lies he there,
And none so poor to do him reverence.
O masters, if I were disposed to stir
Your hearts and minds to mutiny and rage,
I should do Brutus wrong and Cassius wrong,
Who, you all know, are honourable men:
I will not do them wrong; I rather choose
To wrong the dead, to wrong myself and you,
Than I will wrong such honourable men.
But here's a parchment with the seal of Caesar;
I found it in his closet; 'tis his will:

Let but the commons hear this testament
Which, pardon me, I do not mean to read
And they would go and kiss dead Caesar's wounds
And dip their napkins in his sacred blood,
Yea, beg a hair of him for memory,
And, dying, mention it within their wills,
Bequeathing it as a rich legacy
Unto their issue.

The citizens encourage Antony to read Caesar's will.
Antony asks the citizens to gather around Caesar's body and
then he continues:

If you have tears, prepare to shed them now.
You all do know this mantle: I remember
The first time ever Caesar put it on;
'Twas on a summer's evening, in his tent,
That day he overcame the Nervii:
Look, in this place ran Cassius' dagger through:
See what a rent the envious Casca made:
Through this the well-beloved Brutus stabb'd;
And as he pluck'd his cursed steel away,
Mark how the blood of Caesar follow'd it,
As rushing out of doors, to be resolved
If Brutus so unkindly knock'd, or no:
For Brutus, as you know, was Caesar's angel:
Judge, O you gods, how dearly Caesar loved him!
This was the most unkindest cut of all;
For when the noble Caesar saw him stab,
Ingratitude, more strong than traitors' arms,
Quite vanquish'd him: then burst his mighty heart;
And, in his mantle muffling up his face,
Even at the base of Pompey's statua,
Which all the while ran blood, great Caesar fell.
O, what a fall was there, my countrymen!
Then I, and you, and all of us fell down,
Whilst bloody treason flourish'd over us.
O, now you weep, and I perceive you feel
The dint of pity: these are gracious drops.
Kind souls, what! weep you when you but behold
Our Caesar's vesture wounded? Look you here,
Here is himself, marr'd, as you see, with traitors.

This arouses the citizens to violent cries of sorrow and revenge. But Antony is not yet done:

> Good friends, sweet friends, let me not stir you up
> To such a sudden flood of mutiny.
> They that have done this deed are honourable;
> What private griefs they have, alas, I know not,
> That made them do it: they are wise and
> honourable,
> And will, no doubt, with reasons answer you.
> I come not, friends, to steal away your hearts:
> I am no orator, as Brutus is;
> But, as you know me all, a plain blunt man,
> That love my friend; and that they know full well
> That gave me public leave to speak of him:
> For I have neither wit, nor words, nor worth,
> Action, nor utterance, nor the power of speech,
> To stir men's blood: I only speak right on;
> I tell you that which you yourselves do know;
> Show you sweet Caesar's wounds, poor poor dumb
> mouths,
> And bid them speak for me: but were I Brutus,
> And Brutus Antony, there were an Antony
> Would ruffle up your spirits, and put a tongue
> In every wound of Caesar, that should move
> The stones of Rome to rise and mutiny.

The crowd now turns into an angry mob. They seize furniture from the nearby buildings, place Caesar's body on top of this pyre and light it. Then the people, carrying lighted torches, rush off to set fire to the assassins' houses. Antony, satisfied with the effect his speech has created, comments:

> Now let it work. Mischief, thou art afoot,
> Take thou what course thou wilt.

A servant comes to tell Antony that Octavius is already in Rome and awaiting him, with Lepidus, at Caesar's house, and that Brutus and Cassius "Are rid like madmen through the gates of Rome."

A group of angry citizens now comes rushing through the streets and seizes a person who says he is Cinna. They treat him violently, despite his cries that he is Cinna, the poet, not Cinna, the conspirator:

> It is no matter, his name's Cinna; pluck but his name
> out of his heart, and turn him going.

ACT IV

In Antony's house, Antony, Octavius and Lepidus, the triumvirate that now rules Rome, are deciding which Romans must die "by proscription." Antony asks Lepidus to fetch Caesar's will. After Lepidus leaves, Antony remarks that Lepidus is fit only to run errands, but Octavius defends him as an exellent general.

Antony tells Octavius that Brutus and Cassius are organizing armies to challenge the triumvirate, and the three rulers must arrange to meet this challenge. Octavius agrees, adding that they are surrounded by enemies and false friends.

Enough time has passed for the opposing armies to be raised and prepared for battle in Sardis in Asia Minor. Brutus is in his tent, when his officer, Lucilius, returns from his visit to Cassius' approaching army. Lucilius, accompanied by Cassius' servant, Pindarus, brings a letter from Cassius. Brutus reads the letter and then makes the mistake of criticizing Cassius in front of his servant, who defends his master. Brutus makes another mistake when he asks how he was received by Cassius. Lucilius replies:

> With courtesy and with respect enough;
> But not with such familiar instances,
> Nor with such free and friendly conference,
> As he hath used of old.

Brutus' response to this information is, again, criticial:

> Thou hast described
> A hot friend cooling: ever note, Lucilius,
> When love begins to sicken and decay,
> It useth an enforced ceremony.
> There are no tricks in plain and simple faith:
> But hollow men, like horses hot at hand,
> Make gallant show and promise of their mettle;
> But when they should endure the bloody spur,
> They fall their crests and like deceitful jades
> Sink in the trial. Comes his army on?

Then Cassius arrives and greets Brutus. They continue their conversation in Brutus' tent, where Cassius is the first to speak:

That you have wrong'd me doth appear in this:
You have condemn'd and noted Lucius Pella
For taking bribes here of the Sardians;
Wherein my letters, praying on his side,
Because I knew the man, were slighted off.
Brutus: You wrong'd yourself to write in such a case.
Cassius: In such a time as this it is not meet
That every nice offence should bear his comment.
Brutus: Let me tell you, Cassius, you yourself
Are much condemn'd to have an itching palm,
To sell and mart your offices for gold
To undeservers.
Cassius: I an itching palm!
You know that you are Brutus that speaks this,
Or, by the gods, this speech were else your last.
Brutus: The name of Cassius honours this corruption,
And chastisement doth therefore hide his head.
Cassius: Chastisement!
Brutus: Remember March, the ides of March remember:
Did not great Julius bleed for justice' sake?
What villain touch'd his body, that did stab,
And not for justice? What, shall one of us,
That struck the foremost man of all this world
But for supporting robbers, shall we now
Contaminate our fingers with base bribes,
And sell the mighty space of our large honours
For so much trash as may be grasped thus?
I had rather be a dog, and bay the moon,
Than such a Roman.

The accusations about accepting bribes are followed by
further misunderstandings. The argument next turns to the subject of who is the better soldier:

Brutus: You say you are a better soldier:
Let it appear so; make your vaunting true,
And it shall please me well: for mine own part,
I shall be glad to learn of noble men.
Cassius: You wrong me every way; you wrong me,

Brutus;
I said, an elder soldier, not a better;
Did I say, better?
Brutus: If you did, I care not.

Brutus then begins to criticize Cassius' methods of raising money for his troops:

You have done that you should be sorry for.
There is no terror, Cassius, in your threats;
For I am arm'd so strong in honesty,
That they pass by me as the idle wind
Which I respect not. I did send to you
For certain sums of gold, which you denied me:
For I can raise no money by vile means:
By heaven, I had rather coin my heart,
And drop my blood for drachmas, than to wring
From the hard hands of peasants their vile trash
By any indirection. I did send
To you for gold to pay my legions,
Which you denied me: was that done like Cassius?
Should I have answer'd Caius Cassius so?
When Marcus Brutus grows so covetous,
To lock such rascal counters from his friends,
Be ready, gods, with all your thunderbolts,
Dash him to pieces!

Finally, Cassius' old admiration and love for Brutus get the better of him and the two quickly settle their differences:

Cassius: Hath Cassius lived
To be but mirth and laughter to his Brutus,
When grief and blood ill-temper'd vexeth him?
Brutus: When I spoke that, I was ill-temper'd too.
Cassius: Do you confess so much? Give me your hand.
Brutus: And my heart too.

In answer to Cassius' remark about accepting "accidental evils," Brutus reveals that Portia has committed suicide by swallowing hot coals.

28

Impatient of my absence,
And grief that young Octavius with Mark Antony
Have made themselves so strong: for with her death
That tidings came: with this she fell distract,
And, her attendants absent, swallow'd fire.

Lucius enters with the wine, and the two men pledge renewed affection.

The entrance of Titinius and Messala turns their attention to letters received from Rome by Brutus and Messala, reporting the execution of from 70 to 100 senators, including Cicero. Besides this, Messala tells Brutus his letter has reported the death of Portia. This news Brutus seems to receive with a lack of emotion that astonishes Messala, who does not know that Brutus has already been informed. Then they begin to discuss the campaign. Cassius favors waiting for the enemy at Sardis but again he gives in to Brutus, who thinks it would be wisest to advance toward Sardis.

Then Brutus, after sending Lucius for his dressing gown, says good night to the others. Cassius expresses the hope that no arguments will come between them ever again. Lucius returns with the gown. In its pocket, Brutus finds a book he has been looking for. He asks Varro and Claudius to guard his tent and then asks Lucius to play to him while he reads. Noting that Lucius is beginning to fall asleep, Brutus takes the instrument from him and lets him rest.

While Brutus is reading, the ghost of Caesar enters the tent. Brutus looks up from his book and remarks:

How ill this taper burns! Ha! who comes here?
I think it is the weakness of mine eyes
That shapes this monstrous apparition.
It comes upon me. Art thou any thing?
Art thou some god, some angel, or some devil,
That makest my blood cold, and my hair to stare?
Speak to me what thou art.

The ghost tells Brutus that it is his "evil spirit" and that it has come to tell him he shall see it at Philippi. The ghost disappears, and Brutus calls for Lucius and the two sentries. Although they all cried out in their sleep, none can remember having dreamed anything.

ACT V

Brutus and Cassius march with their army to meet Antony and Octavius. The opposing generals meet and begin an extensive parley, after which Antony and Octavius retire with their forces.

Cassius begins telling Messala about things he has seen forewarning evil for their side:

Messala,
This is my birth-day; as this very day
Was Cassius born. Give me thy hand, Messala:
Be thou my witness that, against my will,
As Pompey was, am I compell'd to set
Upon one battle all our liberties.
You know that I held Epicurus strong,
And his opinion: now I change my mind,
And partly credit things that do presage.
Coming from Sardis, on our former ensign
Two mighty eagles fell, and there they perch'd,
Gorging and feeding from our soldiers' hands;
Who to Philippi here consorted us:
This morning are they fled away and gone;
And in their steads do ravens, crows and kites
Fly o'er our heads and downward look on us,
As we were sickly prey: their shadows seem
A canopy most fatal, under which
Our army lies, ready to give up the ghost.

A touching farewell scene between Brutus and Cassius follows:

Now, most noble Brutus,
The goods to-day stand friendly, that we may,
Lovers in peace, lead on our days to age!
But, since the affairs of men rest still incertain,
Let's reason with the worst that may befall.
If we do lose this battle, then is this
The very last time we shall speak together:
What are you then determined to do?
Brutus: Even by the rule of that philosophy
By which I did blame Cato for the death

Which he did give himself: I know not how,
But I do find it cowardly and vile,
For fear of what might fall, so to prevent
The time of life: arming myself with patience
To stay the providence of some high powers
That govern us below.
Cassius: Then, if we lose this battle,
You are contented to be led in triumph
Through the streets of Rome?
Brutus: No, Cassius, no: think not, thou noble
Roman,
That ever Brutus will go bound to Rome;
He bears too great a mind. But this same day
Must end that work the ides of March begun;
And whether we shall meet again I know not.
Therefore our everlasting farewell take.
For ever, and for ever, farewell, Cassius!
If we do meet again, why, we shall smile;
If not, why then this parting was well made.
Cassius: For ever, and for ever, farewell, Brutus!
If we do meet again, we'll smile indeed;
If not, 'tis true this parting was well made.
Brutus: Why then, lead on. O, that a man might
know
The end of this day's business ere it come!
But it sufficeth that the day will end,
And then the end is known. Come, ho! away!

Brutus sends orders by Messala for an attack upon the forces of Octavius, which seem about to give way.

In the meantime, on another part of the field, Cassius' forces are surrounded by Antony's army. Cassius sends Titinius to see whether an approaching troop is theirs or the enemy's and Pindarus to climb a nearby hill to see what happens to Titinius. When Pindarus reports that Titinius appears to be prisoner, Cassius, thinking the enemy is closing in on him, asks Pindarus to kill him. Pindarus stabs Cassius, and, as Cassius falls, he cries, "Caesar, thou art revenged, /Even with the sword that kill'd thee." Pindarus, now free, decides he will run, "Where never Roman shall take note of him."

Titinius enters with Messala. Pindarus had been mistaken; Titinius had met friends who were seeking Cassius to tell him that Brutus had beaten Octavius. Now they find Cassius dead. Messala goes to report to Brutus, while Titinius mourns.

Why didst thou send me forth, brave Cassius?
Did I not meet thy friends? and did not they
Put on my brows this wreath of victory,
And bid me give it thee? Didst thou not hear their shouts?
Alas, thou hast misconstrued every thing!
But, hold thee, take this garland on thy brow;
Thy Brutus bid me give it thee, and I
Will do his bidding. Brutus, come apace,
And see how I regarded Caius Cassius.
By your leave, gods: this is a Roman's part:
Come, Cassius' sword, and find Titinius' heart.

Brutus and Messala return with a group of officers and find both Cassius and Titinius dead. Brutus says:

And yet two Romans living such as these?
The last of all the Romans, fare thee well!
It is impossible that ever Rome
Should breed thy fellow. Friends I owe more tears
To this dead man than you shall see me pay.
I shall find time, Cassius, I shall find time.
Come therefore, and to Thassos send his body:
His funerals shall not be in our camp,
Lest it discomfort us. Lucilius, come,
And come, young Cato: let us to the field.
Labeo and Flavius, set our battles on.
'Tis three o'clock; and, Romans, yet ere night
We shall try fortune in a second fight.

The battle continues. When it seems clear that Brutus is going to be defeated, he tries to persuade two of his friends to kill him. They both refuse and try to persuade him to flee. He tells them good-bye:

Farewell to you; and you; and you, Volumnius.
Strato, thou hast been all this while asleep;
Farewell to thee too, Strato. Countrymen,
My heart doth joy that yet in all my life

I have found no man but he was true to me.
I shall have glory by this losing day,
More than Octavius and Mark Antony
By this vile conquest shall attain unto.
So, fare you well at once; for Brutus' tongue
Hath almost ended his life's history:
Night hangs upon mine eyes; my bones would rest,
That have but labour'd to attain this hour.

Urging the others to escape, Brutus stays behind. He asks Strato to remain and perform one last service:

I prithee, Strato, stay thou by thy lord:
Thou art a fellow of a good respect;
Thy life hath had some smatch of honour in it:
Hold then my sword, and turn away thy face,
While I do run upon it. Wilt thou, Strato?

As Brutus falls upon the sword, he says, "Caesar, now be still: /I kill'd not thee with half so good a will."

Octavius and Antony enter with their prisoners, Messala and Lucilius. Finding Brutus dead, Lucilius rejoices that Brutus will not be taken prisoner. Antony pays tribute to Brutus in a brief, but moving, eulogy:

This was the noblest Roman of them all:
All the conspirators, save only he,
Did that they did in envy of great Caesar;
He only, in a general honest thought
And common good to all, made one of them.
His life was gentle, and the elements
So mix'd in him that Nature might stand up
And say to all the world 'This was a man!'

Octavius declares that Brutus shall be given an honorable soldier's burial. "Let's away," he then suggests, "To part the glories of this happy day."

Part B: Questions and Answers by Act and Scene
ACT I • SCENE I

Question 1.
Summarize the opening scene of the play.

Answer
The play opens in Rome, where the streets are decorated in celebration of Caesar's triumphal return to the city after the defeat of Pompey's sons in battle. Two tribunes, Flavius and Marullus, adopt a stern attitude to a group of workmen for being away from work on what is not an official holiday. The tribunes (officials elected to defend the interests of the people) are obviously sympathizers of the dead Pompey and enemies of Caesar. Their arrogant manner toward the others is characteristic of the hostility existing between aristocrat and commoner. In spite of it, however, the workers are in a holiday mood and freely express their humor in quibbling and punning with the angry tribunes. Marullus and Flavius refer angrily to the fickleness of the people, since it was not long before that Pompey had received their acclaim. Having dismissed the workers, the two tribunes set about dispersing any other crowds to be found in the streets and removing the decorations that, in Caesar's honor, adorn the statues.

Question 2.
What is the purpose of the opening scene?

Answer
The opening scene of the play suggests that there are political factions in Rome; although there is an official celebration to welcome Caesar's homecoming, the two tribunes (and presumably others) are opposed to this.

Some elements of the Roman mob are introduced. Although they are happy in this scene, it is evident from the remarks of Marullus that the temper of the commoners of Rome is changeable.

We are also made slightly familiar with the Roman scene and with some of the important personalities of the present and recent past. Caesar and his defeated enemy, Pompey, are mentioned, and reference is made to the Capitol and to the Tiber River.

Question 3.

Are the citizens who appear in the opening scene of the play typical of a Roman crowd?

Answer

They are really much more characteristic of Londoners in Shakespeare's time. The rule that workers must carry some tool or other indication of their trade with them on Sundays and holidays was typical of Elizabethan England, rather than of ancient Rome. Moreover, these citizens probably are much more free in their speech than Romans would have dared to be. The quibbling and punning, of which they do so much, is also typical of the people of London in the sixteenth century.

Question 4.

What are the reasons for the differing attitudes toward Caesar's triumphant return to Rome, as revealed in the opening scene of the play?

Answer

Triumphal processions through the city had always previously been in celebration of defeated enemies. Pompey and his family were Roman citizens, however, and many people felt that celebrations in such circumstances were in bad taste.

The poorer people tended to praise the hero of the hour, hoping, no doubt, for gifts and favors.

Caesar's personal popularity was feared by many, particularly those with republican sentiments, since it was known that he was ambitious to become king.

ACT I • SCENE 2

Question 1.

Write a summary of Act I, Scene 2, in which Casca tells Cassius and Brutus of the manner in which Caesar was offered a crown by Marc Antony in the Forum.

Answer

Caesar appears under circumstances of pomp and ceremony, accompanied by his associates and followed by a large crowd. The occasion is one of double celebration, since his triumphal homecoming coincides with the annual Feast of the Lupercal. Marc Antony is about to participate in the "running of the course," which forms part of the festival, and Caesar requests him to strike Calphurnia, his wife, during this event. He also tells Calphurnia to be sure to place herself in Antony's path so as to be struck and thus remove her "sterile curse." As the procession continues to the Forum, a soothsayer calls to Caesar to beware the ides of March but is contemptuously dismissed.

Brutus and Cassius stay behind, as they do not wish to be present should a crown be offered to Caesar, as is rumored. Cassius talks excitedly to Brutus of Caesar's ambitions, of how he fears them and how unworthy Caesar is of praise. Brutus, although he likes and respects Caesar personally, is half convinced that Cassius is right.

Shortly afterward, the procession returns, since the festival is now over. Caesar, observing Cassius, tells Marc Antony that he distrusts him. Antony, however, reassures his master.

At Brutus' suggestion, Casca stops to say that Caesar has been offered a crown. He says that the offer was made three times by Marc Antony. On each occasion, Caesar refused it, and the crowd cheered loudly at his apparent reluctance. Caesar then suffered some sort of seizure.

Brutus appears impressed and promises to consider carefully what Cassius has said and to meet him again the next day. Left alone, Cassius reveals his satisfaction that Brutus is partly won over. He then states that he will seek to influence Brutus further by forging letters in different styles of handwriting. Supposedly coming from other persons, these letters will be placed in Brutus' house where they are sure to be found.

Question 2.

What are the main purposes of this scene, in which the Feast of the Lupercal is being celebrated in Rome?

Answer

    a. To introduce the main characters of the play: Julius Caesar, Brutus, Cassius and Marc Antony.

    b. To reveal the proposed conspiracy against Caesar.

    c. To demonstrate the contrast between the jealous and scheming character of Cassius and the honorable, cautious character of Brutus.

 d. To emphasize the physical and mental weaknesses of Caesar's character.

Question 3.
What was the Feast of the Lupercal?

Answer
The Feast of the Lupercal was a festival of purification for the walls of Rome, held annually on February 15. One of its great features was the "course" around the city walls. The race was run by young aristocrats and officials armed with leather thongs, with which they struck the crowd, especially women. It was believed that blows received on this occasion conferred some magical blessing. For this reason, it was the custom for childless matrons to stand in the way, so as to be struck and thereby be "charmed" into motherhood.

Question 4.
Why do Cassius and Brutus leave the company of Caesar and his followers during the celebrations and what do they discuss?

Answer
It has been rumored that a crown may be offered to Caesar, and they do not wish to be present to witness a ceremony with which they disagree in principle. Cassius takes the opportunity to express his bitter resentment and fear of Caesar's ambitions, hinting that Brutus might consider joining a conspiracy to rid Rome of the dictator. Brutus is only partially convinced, but promises to consider the matter.

ACT I • SCENE 3

Question 1.
Outline the main events of Act I, Scene 3.

Answer
A fearsome storm is raging. Cicero and Casca meet in the street, the latter obviously terrified since his sword is drawn. Casca tells a story of fantastic happenings during the storm, but Cicero remains calm. After confirming that Caesar proposes to

attend the senate house the next day, Cicero departs. Cassius then appears and, realizing Casca's state of mind, tells him that the storm is due to the anger of the gods concerning the state of affairs in Rome. He follows this with an angry speech directed against Caesar. The result is that Casca promises to support the conspiracy. Cinna then enters and tells Cassius that he is expected to attend a meeting. Cassius now gives Cinna two forged letters, and instructs him to deliver them to Brutus' house before rejoining the conspirators. Finally, Cassius suggests to Casca that they go to Brutus' house before daylight in a final attempt to win his support for the plot against Caesar.

Question 2.

Suggest the purposes of Act I, Scene 3.

Answer

The purposes of Act I, Scene 3, appear to be as follows:

a. The relating of natural phenomena to human affairs, known as pathetic fallacy, is a traditional device of playwrights. Thus, the violent storm is intended to suggest equally violent political happenings in the immediate future.

b. It provides further evidence, in the matter of Cassius' conversation with Casca and that of the forged letters, of Cassius' skill and determination in the art of persuasion.

c. It demonstrates that Cassius and Cicero, unlike Casca, are not affected by superstitious fears.

d. It shows that the conspiracy is under way and prepares us for the meeting in Brutus' orchard.

Question 3.

What is the purpose of the violent storm, accompanied by fantastic and prophetic events, that occurs in this scene?

Answer

The storm and accompanying events are intended,

a. To produce a tense atmosphere appropriate to conspiracy and lurking violence.

b. To give Cassius the opportunity, by cleverly playing upon the feelings of the frightened Casca, to bring him into the plot.

    c. To give the conspirators the opportunity, since the streets are deserted, to meet secretly and without fear of interruption, in "Pompey's porch."

    d. To cause Brutus to sleep restlessly, so that he will deeply consider the proposed conspiracy.

Question 4.
Describe the actions and reactions of Casca, Cicero and Cinna on the night of the storm.

Answer

Casca is terrified by the storm, but eagerly accepts Cassius' explanation that the weather is due to the anger of the gods concerning the state of affairs in Rome. After listening to further angry remarks by Cassius, Casca agrees to join the conspiracy.

Cicero is not disturbed by the storm, remarking to Casca that "men may construe things after their fashion." His principal concern is whether Caesar will attend the Capitol on the following day.

Cinna is sent by his fellow conspirators to fetch Cassius and, in so doing, he has to go out in the storm, which frightens him badly. On meeting Cassius, the latter laughs at Cinna's fears and sends him to Brutus' house to deliver the forged letters.

Question 5.
How does Cassius, in his soliloquy on the night of the storm, propose to influence Brutus to join the conspiracy?

Answer

He proposes that letters, written in different styles of handwriting and supposedly coming from several citizens, be placed in Brutus' house. All of them will urge Brutus to take part in a movement to rid Rome of Caesar, thereby persuading him that the conspiracy he has been invited to join is a popular one.

ACT II • SCENE 1

Question 1.
Describe the events leading to Brutus' decision to join the conspiracy.

Answer

Brutus passes a sleepless night. This is partly a result of the storm and partly because he is trying to make up his mind whether to join the conspiracy against Caesar. He argues that, although he feels no personal dislike for Caesar, the welfare of the state should be the first consideration. Although Caesar has never been known to act unreasonably, Brutus fears that the absolute power that a crown would give him might change his nature and cause him to play the tyrant.

While Brutus is thinking in his study, his servant brings him a letter that he has found near the window. This letter has been forged by Cassius to persuade Brutus to join the plot. Having read the forged letter, Brutus makes the fateful decision to join the conspirators.

Cassius arrives, bringing with him five associates, who are presented to Brutus formally although he already knows them. In a whispered aside with Cassius, Brutus is presumably offered the leadership of the conspiracy, which he accepts. Cassius appears delighted at his success and does not object to Brutus' refusal to take an oath or the exclusion of Cicero, the orator, from the conspiracy. At Brutus' insistence, it is agreed that the life of Marc Antony shall be spared. Since it is not quite certain that Caesar will attend the senate house in the morning, Decius volunteers to persuade him. Eight o'clock is agreed upon as the time of the assassination, and the conspirators leave.

Portia then enters and complains bitterly that Brutus has appeared moody, preoccupied and impatient lately. She demands to know the cause. Brutus talks to her kindly and agrees to share all his secrets with her.

At this point, Caius Ligarius (having been previously summoned) enters. Without knowing the exact nature of the plot, he agrees, with enthusiasm, to join it.

Question 2.

State the purposes of this scene.

Answer

The apparent objects of the scene in which the conspirators meet in Brutus' orchard are as follows:

    a. To show that Brutus, while persuaded with some reluctance to become the leader of the conspiracy, is determined to be the leader in fact, as well as in name.

b. To suggest that there are serious differences of opinion among the conspirators.

c. To introduce Portia, the wife of Brutus, and thereby lend a note of domesticity to a scene that is otherwise one of serious political manoeuvring.

Question 3.
How does Brutus justify his decision to join the assassins?

Answer
It has been rumored that a crown will be presented to Caesar the next day by the senate. Brutus fears that the absolute power enjoyed by a king could make Caesar a tyrant. He resolves, therefore, that Caesar should be removed before he can do harm.

Question 4.
Explain briefly why Brutus will not permit an oath to be taken by the members of the conspiracy.

Answer
Brutus' reasons for deciding against an oath may be summarized as follows:

a. He is confident of the justness of the plot to rid Rome of Caesar.

b. He believes that an oath is unnecessary and would add no strength to the cause.

c. He believes that the threatened danger to the liberties of Roman citizens should be sufficient motivation to "prick them to redress."

d. An oath would slur the moral character of the conspirators, who supposedly already have the "even virtue of their enterprise."

Question 5.
"No sooner has Brutus consented to become the leader of the conspiracy than he makes it obvious to the others that he means to be the leader in fact, as well as in name." Comment on this statement.

Answer
Brutus soon makes it obvious that he intends to be the real

leader of the conspiracy against Caesar. At his insistence, Cicero, the orator, is given no part in the plot. Moreover, Brutus argues successfully that Marc Antony's life should be spared. It may appear remarkable how, at this early stage, Brutus is able to assume authority over the others, several of whom appear to disagree seriously with him. The reason would appear to be that the conspirators are particularly anxious for him to be their leader, since (unlike some of the others) he is a man of excellent reputation whose leadership will win over many Romans who would otherwise oppose the conspiracy.

Question 6.

Describe the conversation between Brutus and Portia after the conspirators have left.

Answer

Portia complains that Brutus has been preoccupied, impatient, moody and inattentive. As the daughter of one leading Roman (Cato) and the wife of another, she claims the right to know what is troubling him and to share his secrets. To prove that she can bear pain and exercise self-control (and thereby be worthy of his confidence) she has previously wounded herself in the thigh. Brutus is deeply touched by Portia's remarks and promises to confide all his secrets to her.

ACT II • SCENE 2

Question 1.

Describe how Caesar, despite Calphurnia's pleading, is finally persuaded to go to the senate house.

Answer

Caesar has spent a sleepless night and has been further upset by his wife's crying out in her sleep that he is being murdered. Having ordered that the priests offer sacrifices and send him their report, he is joined by his wife, who is in a state of great anxiety. She tells him that he must not leave the house that day and relates in horrible detail the happenings of the night. Caesar is unconvinced and repeats, in pompous terms, his intention of going out. A servant then brings word from the priests that the omens are unfavorable and that Caesar is advised to remain indoors. Caesar remains unconvinced but, in view of Calphurnia's hysterical pleadings, agrees to stay at home. At this point, Decius Brutus enters and is told of Caesar's decision. When he is told why, Decius interprets the dream favorably, speaks flatteringly to Caesar and tells him that the senate is going to offer him a crown, an offer that may be withheld should he not go to the Capitol. Caesar changes his mind once again. A number of senators (most of them conspirators) arrive, and, after the exchange of courtesies, they all depart for the senate house.

Question 2.

Outline the purposes of Act II, Scene 2.

Answer

The probable purposes of the scene in which Caesar is persuaded to go to the senate house are as follows:

a. To present Caesar, because of his superstitious fears and his indecisions, in a somewhat unfavorable light.

b. Caesar's frequent shifts and changes of mind intensify the suspense.

c. The introduction of Calphurnia, Caesar's wife, who pleads urgently with her husband to exercise caution, brings to mind the previous scene, in which Portia demonstrates similar concern for Brutus. At this stage, therefore, the audience realizes quite clearly that two of the principal figures of the drama have a private, as well as a public, life.

Question 3.

What factors probably influence Caesar to ignore his fears about attending the meeting of the Senate that day?

Answer

Caesar is probably influenced by the fear of being thought afraid by his people, the notion that he is semi-divine and therefore immune to harm, Decius Brutus' interpretation of Calphurnia's dream to the satisfaction of Caesar and Decius Brutus' statement that the senate has decided to offer Caesar a crown that day and that, if he fails to attend, the offer may be reconsidered.

Question 4.

Account for Caesar's pompous and arrogant language during the scene when he is making up his mind whether or not to attend the senate.

Answer

It is possible to excuse Caesar's arrogance when he is making up his mind whether he should attend the senate house. Caesar, in common with most Romans, is somewhat superstitious by nature. To some extent, he appears to share the fears and anxieties displayed by his wife. However, his natural pride and bravery are in conflict with his superstitious fears. It may be that he is trying, by his arrogant remarks, to stimulate in himself the confidence that he apparently lacks. It is as though Caesar is temporarily overcome by the grandeur and importance of his position as the leader of the Roman state.

ACT II • SCENE 3

Question 1.

Describe what happens in this brief scene.

Answer

This scene reveals that the conspiracy is in danger of betrayal. Artemidorus, a teacher of rhetoric, has somehow learned of the plot. He stands in a street near the Capitol with a letter, which he reads out aloud. It is addressed to Caesar and mentions eight of the conspirators by name. Artemidorus proposes to wait in a convenient place until Caesar approaches and then to hand him the letter, pretending that it is an urgent petition.

ACT II • SCENE 4

Question 1.

State the function and outline the events of this scene.

Answer

This scene fills in the interval between Caesar's departure from his home and his arrival at the senate house.

It is evident, from Portia's extreme anxiety on her husband's account that Brutus has confided to her the details of the conspiracy. She is so agitated that she cannot await the outcome, but sends the boy, Lucius, to the Capitol with instructions to find out how Brutus is and what Caesar is doing. The soothsayer enters and, on being questioned by Portia, reveals that he is about to warn Caesar of approaching danger. The remarks of the soothsayer serve to increase her fears. In her distress, she makes an indiscreet remark, but qualifies it quickly and sends Lucius on his errand.

Question 2.
What evidence is there in Act II, Scene 4, that Brutus has confided the details of the conspiracy to his wife, Portia?

Answer
Portia's knowledge of the conspiracy is shown in her extreme distress before the assassination takes place and in her remark, "O Brutus, /The heavens speed thee in thine enterprise," which she attempts to cover up.

Question 3.
What purposes are served by the scenes (Act II, Scenes 3 and 4) in which it is revealed that Artemidorus and the soothsayer plan to warn Caesar on his way to the Capitol?

Answer
The purposes of the suggestion that Caesar is about to be warned by two different persons, acting independently, are several:

a. The suspense is heightened, since the audience does not know whether they will succeed in attracting Caesar's attention and, if so, whether he will listen to their warnings.

b. The remarks of the soothsayer to Portia serve to increase her anxieties. As a result, she makes an indiscreet remark to Lucius. Had the boy heard and understood her, she might have been the unwitting cause of her husband's betrayal. Thus, again, the suspense is raised.

c. Portia's almost frantic behavior is in marked contrast to her behavior in Brutus' orchard when she demands to know her husband's confidences. The audience is thus made aware of the weaker side of her nature.

ACT III • SCENE 1

Question 1.
Summarize the events leading to and immediately following the murder of Caesar.

Answer
This scene contains, in the murder of Caesar, the climax of the play. On his way to the senate house, Caesar exchanges words with the soothsayer, but ignores his warning. Artemidorus then presents Caesar with his "petition," but Decius quickly steps in front of him with another petition, from Trebonius. Despairingly, Artemidorus cries out that his letter is of vital concern, but he is disregarded. When the group arrives at the senate house, there is some slight fear that the conspiracy will be betrayed by Popilius. However, Caesar smiles when talking to Popilius, indicating that the latter reveals nothing of the plot. Trebonius then takes Marc Antony outside on some excuse, so that he cannot interfere. At this point, Metellus Cimber, with exaggerated humility, kneels in front of Caesar's chair. Caesar, presuming that Metellus is trying to plead for his banished brother, refuses his appeal in arrogant and pompous terms. Brutus, Cassius, Cinna and Decius then pretend to reinforce Metellus' suit, but are all denied. Casca then stabs Caesar and is followed by the rest of the conspirators, with Brutus striking last. Cinna and Cassius cry out hysterically of liberty and freedom, and the senators escape hurriedly. The assassins then exchange pleasantries and wash their hands in Caesar's blood. Their intention is to go to the Forum to justify their act to the citizens.

They are interrupted, however, by a servant sent by Marc Antony, who was supposed to have fled in terror. The servant requests safe-conduct for his master, who wishes to meet Brutus and the rest. Marc Antony appears shortly afterward. Antony is grief-stricken and offers to share the same fate as Caesar, should the plotters wish to kill him also. He is reassured by Brutus and Cassius and is promised a complete explanation after the citizens have been quieted. Having shaken hands with Caesar's murderers, Antony then loses his self-control and delivers an impassioned eulogy of his dead master. Upon being questioned by Cassius about his intentions, he again expresses his friendship for the conspirators, provided that he is given the reasons for the deed. Once again, he is given this assurance.

Antony then requests permission to speak at Caesar's funeral. Cassius objects to this suggestion but he is overruled by Brutus, provided that a number of conditions are fulfilled. Marc Antony agrees. Left to himself, he asks pardon of Caesar's corpse for his apparent approval of the murder. He then predicts civil war.

A servant of Octavius Caesar appears, saying that his master is 25 miles from Rome. After some thought, Antony decides to detain the servant until after his speech in the Forum the next day, when he will send him back to Octavius to report the temper of the citizens. The scene closes with the servant helping Antony to remove Caesar's corpse.

Question 2.
What purposes are served by the assassination scene?

Answer
- *a.* The conspirators achieve their goal — the murder of Caesar.
- *b.* Brutus, Cassius and the rest are shown to disagree about Antony and reveal their inability to take appropriate measures to control a dangerous situation.
- *c.* The audience is prepared for the funeral ceremonies, in which both Brutus and Antony will figure.
- *d.* The appearance of Octavius Caesar, who obviously will oppose the conspirators, is foreshadowed.

Question 3.
Why, on his way to the Capitol, does Caesar not read the petition handed to him by Artemidorus?

Answer
Caesar does not read the petition because Decius quickly steps ahead of Artemidorus to present another petition from Trebonius and because Artemidorus tells Caesar that his petition deals with a personal matter, which leads Caesar to reply, "What touches us ourself shall last be served."

Question 4.
What parts do Trebonius, Metellus Cimber and Casca play in the murder of Caesar?

Answer
Trebonius causes Antony, on some excuse, to leave the scene, Metellus presents a petition on Caesar in fawning terms to distract his attention and Casca strikes the first blow by stabbing Caesar in the neck.

Question 5.
Describe the scene immediately after the assassination of Caesar.

Answer
The senators and other people present run in confusion. Cinna and Cassius shout out hysterically about liberty and freedom. Brutus makes an unsuccessful attempt to prevent the general panic, with the object, presumably, of explaining the reasons for the murder. The conspirators then wash their hands in Caesar's blood.

Question 6.
How does Marc Antony approach the conspirators after the murder of Caesar?

Answer
Through his servant, Antony requests safe-conduct, so that he may speak with the conspirators. When he appears, he is assured by Brutus and Cassius that he will not be harmed and he is promised a full explanation of Caesar's murder once the people have been calmed. After shaking hands with all present, Antony breaks into a passionate eulogy of Caesar, but is interrupted by Cassius, who is suspicious. Cassius demands to know whether Antony is to be regarded as friend or enemy. Antony is half apologetic and says that he wishes to be friendly to all, on the condition that the murder be explained to his satisfaction. This is agreed, and Antony then asks to make a speech at Caesar's funeral. Cassius protests, but Brutus consents, provided that the five following conditions are observed:
- *a.* Antony's speech must follow that of Brutus.
- *b.* The conspirators must not be blamed.
- *c.* Antony must speak favorably of Caesar.
- *d.* Antony must state that he is speaking with the conspirators' permission.

e. Antony must speak from the same platform as Brutus. Antony agrees to these conditions.

ACT III • SCENE 2

Question 1.
Write an outline of this scene, in which Brutus and Marc Antony speak at Caesar's funeral ceremonies.

Answer

Brutus and Cassius appear in the Forum, where an excited mob awaits an explanation of Caesar's assassination. The people are angrily demanding satisfaction, and Brutus feels it wise to reduce their numbers by sending some of them away with Cassius, while the rest stay and listen to his speech. Brutus delivers a coldly logical speech, appealing purposely to the reason of the people and deliberately avoiding stirring their emotions. The citizens are impressed and praise Brutus as a deliverer. Brutus then announces that Marc Antony will speak, with the permission of the conspirators.

Antony's speech is entirely different from that of Brutus. Realizing that, at first, the mob is mildly hostile, he makes use of every possible speaking device—pathos, emphasis, apostrophe, repetition and irony. Showing them Caesar's will, he pretends that he should not read it because it may turn them against the conspirators. He then goes on to display Caesar's robe, identifying the various holes in it with the individual murderers. Having by now roused the people to a peak of excitement, he finally reads to them the provisions of Caesar's will, by which all of them benefit. The crowd, by this time, has become an unreasoning mob. Brutus' calm, rational words are forgotten, and the effects of Antony's emotional appeal become apparent. The people run off in a violent mood, evidently planning to avenge the death of Caesar.

A servant enters, telling Antony that Octavius is in Rome. Self-confident as a result of the success of his speech, Antony orders the servant to accompany him to the house of Lepidus, where Octavius is staying.

Question 2.
What are the purposes of the funeral scene?

Answer
a. The emotional speech of Antony is contrasted starkly with the reasoned, logical address of Brutus.
b. Marc Antony, by his emotional speech, gains sway over the Roman mob, thus suggesting that the conspirators' success may be short-lived.
c. The fickleness of the Roman mob is revealed. At first, Brutus is the popular hero until Antony turns them against him.
d. The formation of an alliance, consisting of Antony, Octavius and Lepidus, is foreshadowed.

Question 3.
Why does Marc Antony's speech during Caesar's funeral ceremony have a much more powerful effect on the crowd than Brutus' speech?

Answer
Since Marc Antony's speech follows that of Brutus, he has the last word. Although Antony follows the rules imposed on him by Brutus, he makes effective use of several devices of oratory to successfully condemn the conspirators. Finally, he reminds the people of Caesar's services to the state and, with apparent hesitancy, reads the terms of Caesar's will.

Question 4.
Describe the immediate outcome of Marc Antony's speech.

Answer
The mob is angered, and an orgy of looting and destruction follows. The conspirators flee from the city. A triumvirate is formed to take Caesar's place. It consists of Octavius, Antony and Lepidus.

ACT III • SCENE 3

Question 1.
Outline the purposes of this scene, in which Cinna, the poet, is mistaken for Cinna, the conspirator.

Answer
It demonstrates clearly how successful Antony's speech has

been. It shows that a mob acts without reason, since, in this scene, an innocent man (Cinna, the poet) is murdered. It also illustrates the grim humor of the playwright concerning a fellow writer ("Tear him for his bad verses").

ACT IV • SCENE 1

Question 1.
Write a summary of the proscription scene, in which the members of the triumvirate appear for the first time in the play.

Answer
The members of the triumvirate meet in a house in Rome to discuss their plan of action against the conspirators and their followers. They draw up a list of proscriptions—persons to be outlawed, whom anyone may kill. Marc Antony sends Lepidus to Caesar's house to bring back his will. After Lepidus' departure, Antony takes the opportunity of speaking critically of him to Octavius, suggesting that he can be relieved of his responsibilities, leaving the affairs of state to the other two. Octavius, however, is not convinced and defends Lepidus as a brave soldier. The scene closes with the resolution that, since Brutus and Cassius are raising troops, the triumvirate must do everything possible to discover treachery among its supporters and to meet the coming challenge.

Question 2.
Outline the purposes of Act IV, Scene 1.

Answer
   a. Octavius Caesar, the nephew and heir of Julius Caesar, makes his first appearance in the play.
   b. There is some disagreement among the triumvirs, a fact that casts some doubts upon their eventual success and thereby heightens the tension.
   c. The ruthlessness of Roman political leaders is revealed in the drawing up of the proscription list.
   d. Marc Antony reveals himself in a less pleasant light than in his earlier appearances.

Question 3.

What unpleasant aspects of Marc Antony's character are revealed in the proscription scene?

Answer

Since, at this time, Antony is the dominant member of the triumvirate, he must take most of the blame for the notorious proscription. He talks of reducing the bequests of Caesar's will and he talks disparagingly to Octavius of Lepidus, with the object of eliminating Lepidus from the triumvirate.

ACT IV • SCENE 2

Question 1.

State what happens in this brief scene.

Answer

This short scene introduces us to Brutus' camp at Sardis. Cassius is approaching with his troops, and the two leaders are about to join forces after an extensive recruiting campaign. Lucilius returns from a visit to Cassius' army, carrying a letter to Brutus from his friend. Brutus reads it and then speaks bitterly of Cassius' recent behavior. Pindarus, Cassius' servant, who accompanies Lucilius, defends his master firmly but courteously. Brutus then goes on to question Lucilius as to Cassius' manner toward him, and receives the reply that he has been treated less warmly than formerly. Cassius appears and, without formal greeting, accuses Brutus of having treated him unjustly. Brutus denies this and tells him that they must not quarrel openly in front of their troops. The soldiers are led away a short distance, and the two leaders enter Brutus' tent to continue their discussion privately.

Question 2.

What is the purpose of the scene at Sardis when Cassius rejoins Brutus? What does it foreshadow?

Answer

It serves to reveal the existence of tension between Brutus and Cassius, a fact comparable to the division among leaders of the opposing armies. It also shows both Brutus and Cassius in angry moods and, therefore, prepares the audience for the bitter quarrel between them that forms the subject of the next scene.

ACT IV • SCENE 3

Question 1.
Outline the stages of the quarrel between Brutus and Cassius.

Answer

a. Cassius accuses Brutus of punishing one of his friends for accepting bribes in Sardis, despite Cassius' defence of his friend.

b. Brutus replies that Cassius' attempt to defend such an offence is dishonorable.

c. Cassius argues that a trivial offence should go unnoticed, since they are not living in ordinary times.

d. Cassius loses his temper and implies that he would have killed anyone else who might have accused him of such corruption.

e. Brutus goes on to say that if anyone but Cassius had been guilty, he would have been punished. He then reminds Cassius that Caesar was killed for the sake of justice and that if they, the conspirators, act dishonorably, they are guilty of inconsistency.

f. Cassius says that he is the elder soldier of the two and is, therefore, better able to decide such questions as the method of raising money for war purposes and of promotions.

g. After further quarrelling, Brutus refers (mistakenly) to Cassius' statement that he is the better soldier, and asks him to prove it, since he is always ready to be taught by abler men.

h. Cassius accuses Brutus of being unjust to him, saying that he did not boast of being an abler soldier, but rather an elder one.

i. Brutus ignores Cassius' explanation and proceeds (inconsistently) to scold Cassius for not having sent him funds when he needed them.

j. Cassius denies this and explains that the misunderstanding was due to the stupidity of a messenger.

k. After some further exchanges, Cassius draws his dagger

and urges Brutus to stab him, if he really considers him blameworthy.

l. Brutus tells Cassius to put away his dagger and he apologizes for his hastiness. A reconciliation follows.

Question 2.

Suggest the purposes of Act IV, Scene 3, in which Brutus and Cassius quarrel bitterly and the ghost of Caesar appears in Brutus' tent.

Answer

a. The violent and bitter quarrel between Brutus and Cassius reveals their fundamentally different temperaments and attitudes.

b. Brutus asserts his dominance over Cassius in the matter of meeting the enemy at Philippi. In spite of the misgivings of Cassius, the more experienced military leader, Brutus' plan is adopted.

c. The appearance of Caesar's ghost arouses the notion that Caesar may perhaps be avenged and the conspirators punished in the forthcoming battle with the forces of the triumvirate.

Question 3.

Describe the circumstances of the appearance of Caesar's ghost, the reactions of Brutus and the probable effects of the episode on the minds of the audience.

Answer

On the night before the battle of Philippi, Brutus is reading in his tent, in dim candlelight. A vague shape approaches, startling him. He challenges the spirit, which tells him that it is his evil genius and that it will appear again at Philippi.

Brutus' immediate reaction is one of fear. His remarks to the ghost are brief and he appears calm, but, after the ghost's disappearance, he indicates that he would have wished further conversation with it. He then wakes up the other persons in the tent, who, although they have been crying out in their sleep, deny any knowledge of the ghost's visit.

The effect of Caesar's ghost on the audience probably would be to remind them that Caesar, although dead, still exerts some influence on continuing events and that the eventual victory of Brutus and Cassius is in doubt.

ACT V • SCENE 1

Question 1.
Describe the opening scene of this act.

Answer
The scene opens with Marc Antony and Octavius at Philippi, discussing the intentions of the enemy. The latter appear, and there is a short parley, characterized by the exchange of bitter insults and accusations between the rival commanders. Octavius and Marc Antony then leave to take up their positions. Cassius talks gloomily to Messala, mentioning the numerous omens seen during the march from Sardis. Brutus vows to Cassius that he will not allow himself to be taken prisoner should they lose the battle. The scene ends with Brutus and Cassius saying farewell to each other in case they never meet again.

Question 2.
Describe the difference of opinion between Marc Antony and Octavius.

Answer
The difference of opinion between Marc Antony and Octavius concerns the relative positions their respective bodies of troops are to occupy in the forthcoming battle. Antony, because of his age and experience, has formerly been in undisputed military command. Octavius, however, attempts to assert his personal authority as the heir of Julius Caesar and annoys Antony by reminding him how he wrongly predicted Brutus' course of action. Antony wishes Octavius and his men to take the left side of the plain. Octavius, however, insists on taking the right side. When asked by Antony why he must defy his wishes, Octavius gives an ambiguous reply that may mean either that he is not opposing Antony or that he will oppose Antony on a later occasion.

Question 3.

Show that, before the Battle of Philippi, both Brutus and Cassius sense their coming defeat and deaths.

Answer

Cassius criticizes Brutus, saying that he should not have spared Antony's life. Then Cassius speaks gloomily to Messala about the unfavorable omens encountered on the road from Sardis. He goes on to express his fears that the success of their entire enterprise should be staked on the outcome of a single battle. Brutus tells Cassius that he will not return to Rome as a captive and that he will commit suicide if they lose the battle. Finally, Brutus and Cassius say good-bye to each other in an emotional manner.

ACT V • SCENE 2

Question 1.

What is the purpose of this short scene and the ones that follow?

Answer

The effective presentation of successive battle actions on the stage is a matter of extreme difficulty. However, Shakespeare overcomes the problem by having a sequence of brief scenes, each one portraying a small part of the battlefield and the limited action taking place there. By means of this device, the audience receives a definite impression of individual events and their relationship to the plot as a whole.

ACT V • SCENE 3

Question 1.

Outline the events that occur in this scene.

Answer

Cassius' troops are in a state of panic. Cassius tells Titinius that he has killed his standard-bearer because he was about to flee. Pindarus, the servant, arrives to tell his master that their camp has been taken by Marc Antony. They go to a nearby hill and observe the camp in flames. Cassius, seeing a body of troops in the distance, sends Titinius to find out whether they are friend or enemy. Since his eyesight is poor, he then instructs Pindarus to go to the top of the hill to see what he can. Pindarus reports that Titinius, having been pursued by mounted troops, has been surrounded by them and that they are shouting in triumph. Cassius then calls Pindarus from the hilltop and reminds him that, when he took him prisoner in Parthia, he spared his life on the condition that he should obey all orders. He then orders the slave to stab him. Pindarus does so and flees.

Titinius and Messala appear and find the corpse of Cassius. They realize that there has been some misunderstanding, but do not realize that Pindarus mistook Messala and his men for the enemy. Messala leaves to take the news to Brutus. Titinius remains behind, supposedly to look for Pindarus. Once alone, he stabs himself. Brutus arrives and grieves deeply for the death of his friend. He then makes arrangements for Cassius' corpse to be sent to Thasos for burial and he returns to take command of his troops in the next fight.

ACT V • SCENE 4

Question 1.
What is the probable purpose of the introduction of young Cato in the last act of the play?

Answer
Young Cato, son of the famous Cato, and Brutus' brother-in-law, appears in this act as a fanatical youth. He shouts out his name, and that of his illustrious father, protesting his true patriotism. It would appear, from his extreme and bold language, that he is almost determined to be killed. The purpose of his appearance is apparently to show the defeat of true republicanism (which he and his family represent) and the triumph of the opposing side (as evidenced by the victory of Octavius Caesar).

ACT V • SCENE 5

Question 1.
Write an outline of the final scene of the play, in which Brutus commits suicide.

Answer

By now, Brutus is certain of defeat. He is last seen in a deserted corner of the battlefield with four of his followers. He asks three of them, in turn, to hold his sword so that he may fall on it. Since they are his loyal friends, they refuse. An alarm sounds, and Brutus is left alone with Strato. The latter reluctantly agrees to do what his three comrades have declined. Brutus and Strato shake hands, Strato holds the sword and Brutus falls on it and dies. Octavius and Marc Antony then appear and find Brutus' body. Both of them deliver eulogies praising Brutus' personal honor and bravery.

Question 2.

Indicate the significance of the final scene of the play.

Answer

a. The last of the conspirators are defeated and killed.
b. The tragic denouement is shown as the inevitable consequence, not of wickedness, but of a noble error of judgment.
c. It marks the end of the old-fashioned spirit and practice of republicanism in Rome.
d. It shows Octavius as the inheritor of all that Julius Caesar had created and the representative of the Caesarism that the conspirators had utterly failed to suppress. It is fitting, therefore, that Octavius should make the last speech.

Question 3.

In what ways is the nobility of Brutus' character stressed in the final scene of the play?

Answer

His nobility is stressed by the refusal of Dardanius, Clitus and Volumnius to help him to commit suicide because of their love for him; his last words, in which he states that he takes his own life with less reluctance than he did that of Caesar; and the spontaneous tributes of both Marc Antony and Octavius to his uprightness of character.

Part C: General Review Questions and Answers

Question 1.

Write a brief account of the historical background of the play.

Answer

Julius Caesar was born in 102 B.C. and died the victim of an assassination plot, in 44 B.C. During Caesar's early years, life in Rome was characterized by civil strife between democratic elements, led by Marius, and aristocratic elements, led by Sulla with the support of the senate. The outcome was rarely very clear, since each leader, in turn, assumed charge of affairs, according to the varying fortunes of war. After the death of Marius in 87 B.C., Sulla attempted to make the authority of the senate supreme. After Sulla's death in 78 B.C., Pompey assumed the leadership of the aristocratic elements and rapidly became very popular, largely as a result of his firmness and success in dealing with public affairs, both at home and abroad.

Meanwhile, Julius Caesar was also becoming a popular and successful figure in Roman affairs. In 60 B.C., the first triumvirate was established, consisting of Pompey, Caesar and Crassus, a wealthy and influential Roman.

In 59 B.C., after his election as consul, Caesar, realizing that military advancement was a certain method of obtaining power and prestige, made sure he received the title of pro-consul (military governor) of Gaul. During the next eight years, from 58 to 50 B.C., he carried out a series of successful military campaigns in Britain and Gaul.

After the death of Crassus in 53 B.C., the first triumvirate was dissolved, and a spirit of jealous rivalry developed between Pompey and Caesar. Eventually, the senate, which was opposed to the growing power of Caesar (especially since he was identified with the more democratic elements of the population), supported Pompey and ordered Caesar back to Rome.

Caesar, however, disobeyed the orders of the senate and marched on Italy from Gaul, with the intention of imposing his will on Pompey and the senate. Pompey and his supporters departed hurriedly for the east. In the following year, Caesar defeated his enemies at the Battle of Pharsalus, in Thessaly. Pompey then took refuge in Egypt, where he was later assassinated, in the year 48 B.C., by one of his own followers.

Pompey's sons, Cneius and Sextus, continued the struggle against Julius Caesar but were eventually overwhelmed at the Battle of Munda, in Spain, which was characterized by great violence and enormous casualties on both sides.

The play opens at the point at which Caesar is returning in triumph from the Battle of Munda. It is noteworthy that the occasion of his triumph was not the defeat of a foreign enemy, but of fellow countrymen—the supporters of Pompey, his former colleague.

Question 2.
What are the sources of the play?

Answer
Plutarch, a Greek student of classical history, who lived in the second century A.D., wrote a number of *Parallel Lives*, in which he contrasted the careers and achievements of selected pairs of heroes, one of each pair being a Greek and the other a Roman. A popular French translation of Plutarch's works was made by Amyot in 1559. This was translated into English in 1579, and a second edition was published in 1595. It was probably the latter edition that Shakespeare used as the source for *Julius Caesar*. The central parts of the drama appear to have been borrowed directly from Plutarch's accounts of Caesar and Brutus, while some minor matters come from those of Marcus Antonius and Cicero. In general, Shakespeare appears to have followed Plutarch closely. The main differences lie in the characterization of some of the leading figures of the drama.

Question 3.
In what ways does the play depart from historical truth?

Answer
It should be realized that a dramatist, dealing with happenings that extend over a long period, must shorten the time and compress the facts. Otherwise, a historical play would appear fragmentary and lacking in continuity. Substantially, *Julius Caesar* is true to history, although Shakespeare found it necessary to sacrifice accuracy in certain details. Because of his poetic insight, he was able to enter into the spirit of Roman affairs. The play, therefore, gives a vivid picture of the period

and crisis with which it deals. The principal departures from historical truth are as follows:

a. The Cassius of the play is represented as a nobler character than the Cassius of history.

b. The Brutus of the play is apparently a closer friend of Caesar than was actually so; thus, his participation in the assassination plot is seemingly more shocking and unnatural.

c. Caesar's triumphal entry into Rome actually occurred in October, 45 B.C. Shakespeare advances the incident so that it coincides with the Feast of the Lupercal in February 44 B.C.

d. Shakespeare's statement that Cicero "will never follow anything that other men begin" is largely a matter of supposition. Yet it is believable and suggests a valid reason why Cicero should not be admitted to the circle of conspirators.

e. According to the play, the murder, the reading of the will, the funeral ceremonies and Octavius' arrival in Rome all occur on the same day. Historically, the murder took place on March 15, the will was published on March 18 and the funeral ceremonies took place on March 19 or 20, while Octavius did not return to Rome until May.

f. Caesar was actually murdered in the Curia Pompeiana, not in the Capitol.

g. The words, "et tu, Brute," do not occur in Plutarch. They appear to have been something of a stage commonplace in Shakespeare's time.

h. There is no historical authority for the conditions under which Brutus permits Antony to speak at the funeral ceremonies.

i. The play gives the impression that the triumvirs, meeting in Rome, do so almost immediately after the murder. In fact, they met near Bologna, in November, 43 B.C., more than a year-and-a-half afterwards, following months of civil war among themselves.

j. From the play, it would appear that Antony contemplates tampering with the terms of Caesar's will. In fact, Antony seized much of the money left by Caesar, and the distribution of what was left was arranged by Octavius.

k. The conversation between Brutus and Cassius concerning the coming battle is represented by Plutarch as having taken place at Philippi (not Sardis) immediately before the battle.

l. Historically, Octavius commanded the left wing of the army at the Battle of Philippi, not the right wing, as Shakespeare indicates.

m. Shakespeare combines the two battles of Philippi. In fact, there was an interval of 20 days between them. Cassius died in the first battle (in which Octavius was too ill to participate) and Brutus died after the second.

Question 4.

What is an anachronism? How do anachronisms occur? Mention some examples in the play.

Answer

An anachronism is an error of chronology, especially one that dates an event or object before its correct time. Anachronisms are fairly common in Shakespeare's plays and may be due either to ignorance of the correct facts or to necessity, so as to avoid inconsistency. In Elizabethan times, there was little or no stage scenery, while period costumes had not yet been introduced. It would have been ridiculous, therefore, for characters to refer to articles of clothing that they were not wearing.

The following are some examples of anachronisms:

a. Flavius' reference to "the sign of your profession" is most likely an allusion to the regulations of the Elizabethan trade guilds, which required that workers carry a tool of their trade on holidays. (Act I, Scene 1)

b. Caesar is wearing a doublet—an article of sixteenth-century dress (Act I, Scene 2).

c. Cassius and Decius speak of glasses. In Roman times, the mirror was made of polished metal mirrors (Act I, Scene 2; Act II, Scene 1).

d. The conspirators are wearing wide-brimmed hats. The Romans did not wear these (Act II, Scene 1).

e. Calphurnia speaks of "the horrid sights seen by the watch" (Act II, Scene 2). Shakespeare was thinking of the London of his own day. In fact, night watchmen were not established in Rome before the rule of Augustus Caesar.

f. Brutus speaks twice of striking clocks. Clocks had not been invented in Roman times (Act II, Scene 2).

g. Antony says that "the good is oft interred with their bones" (Act III, Scene 2), while Octavius speaks of "all respect and rites of burial" (Act V, Scene 5). In fact, cremation was the general custom in ancient Rome.

h. Cassius comments, "How vilely doth this cynic rime" (Act IV, Scene 3). In Caesar's time, rhyme was not a feature of Roman poetry.

i. Pockets were not worn in the Roman gown (toga) until some centuries later (Act IV, Scene 3).

Question 5.
How was suicide regarded in ancient Rome?

Answer
In Ancient Rome (as in Japan in modern times), suicide was commonly regarded as an honorable method of escaping the consequences of personal defeat and disgrace. Fear of death was considered to be a dishonorable sentiment. In Roman times, it was apparently not uncommon for sick and aged people to commit suicide to relieve others of the burden of their support. Slaves and servants, in the manner of Hindu widows, sometimes displayed their devotion to their masters by choosing to die with them, or shortly afterward, during the funeral rites. Others might kill themselves from motives of personal vanity, in an attempt to gain the fame that an ordinary or uneventful life had failed to bring them.

"Death before dishonor" was a belief widely held in Roman times, and, to many a Roman, failure and dishonor were synonymous. Even the Stoics (of whom Brutus was one) appeared to follow the practice of suicide, although less freely. They apparently only resorted to it when there was no other possible means of avoiding dishonor or humiliating defeat.

Question 6.
Brutus was a Stoic, and Cassius an Epicurean. What were the principal ideas of these two conflicting philosophies?

Answer

According to the philosophy of Stoicism, the supreme end of life is virtue, which must seek expression in action. True wisdom results in the performance of duty. The wise man, while not lacking feeling, should act without passion and, in doing his duty, should spare neither himself nor others. Joy, grief, pain and pleasure, since they are part of the normal human experience, should be endured without any show of emotion. In controversial matters, each man is his own judge of what is best.

According to Epicurean philosophy, pleasure and the pursuit of pleasure are the principal ends of life. Man's first concern is to free the body from pain and the soul from anxiety. For this reason, therefore, overindulgence is to be avoided and moderation in all things is advised. Fear, and particularly the fear of death, are believed to be the greatest evils. These may be overcome by living a full and happy life in the material world.

Question 7.

Write a character sketch of Brutus.

Answer

Brutus is an idealist and a philosopher, essentially upright and noble in character, but somewhat self-righteous, scholarly and unpractical. He is a Stoic with lofty theories about life and human nature, but he possesses little true insight into realities. Under the self-restraint that characterizes him, his personality is tender and sensitive. He is a bookish man and a theorist. When faced with the necessity for action, rather than theorizing or contemplation, he is revealed as inept.

The uprightness of his character is apparent throughout the play. Even in the matter of Caesar's assassination, Brutus is able to satisfy us that his motives are pure, that his action is without bitterness and that the matter is considered in the light of the "general good." To a great extent, Brutus is the tool of those he leads. The prime responsibility for the plot is assigned to him, since it is felt that his reputation for honesty will lend an air of righteousness to the schemes of the assassins. However, once Brutus has assumed the leadership of the conspiracy, it quickly becomes apparent that he will not be content with the mere pretence of leadership, but that he intends to be the leader in fact, as well as in name. Indeed, it is due to his dominance, particularly in military matters, over the more experienced

Cassius, that the conspirators' worst blunders are made. Brutus' deficiencies stem from his great fault in supposing it to be his duty to interfere with matters that he only partly understands. Added to this is the fact that the characters of his accomplices are so inferior to his that he cannot appreciate their true natures. A man so lacking in insight and judgment where other men and their motives are concerned is doomed to failure when he exchanges the role of rational philosopher for that of statesman and military leader.

Question 8.

"While the name of the play is *Julius Caesar*, the tragic hero is really Brutus." Comment on this statement.

Answer

The greatness of Caesar is largely impressed on the audience by the following:

a. His triumphal procession on returning to Rome (Act I, Scene 2).

b. Marc Antony's speeches:

O mighty Caesar! dost thou lie so low?
Are all thy conquests, glories, triumphs, spoils,
Shrunk to this little measure?

(Act III, Scene 1)

Thou art the ruins of the noblest man
That ever lived in the tide of times.

(Act III, Scene 1)

The whole of Marc Antony's speech in the Forum during the funeral ceremonies.

(Act III, Scene 2).

c. The several references to the spirit of Caesar (Act I, Scene 2; Act II, Scene 1; Act III, Scene 1; Act V, Scene 3; Act V, Scene 5).

However, it might be argued that Cassius' severe attacks on Caesar (Act I, Scene 2) are sufficiently strong in tone to counteract the later eulogies of Marc Antony. While the spirit of Caesar pervades the drama, a spirit (even that of Caesar) cannot be regarded in the same light as a living hero. As for Caesar himself, he speaks only 123 lines altogether, and many of these reveal him in a less than favorable light.

By contrast with Caesar, Brutus is seen to be a scholar, a philosopher and a man of unquestionable principle. But he is, unfortunately, an ineffective and indecisive leader. He possesses the marked advantage that Shakespeare appears to sympathize with and approve of his scruples and inconsistencies. These are to be regarded as unforgivable in a leader of little experience—and one, however, who is determined to lead, no matter how incompetently. Caesar is murdered early in the third act of the play, and Brutus has the advantage that he holds our interest until the final scene of the drama.

Character appears to be the basis of action in all Shakespearean tragedies, and it seems that the playwright was more interested in his characters and their motives than in plot or theme. It has been said that Shakespeare's main purpose in writing this play was to demonstrate that the highest motives and the loftiest principles are insufficient to transform evil into good. Viewed from this standpoint, it is evident that Brutus is the tragic hero. Moreover, while Caesar was both a great statesman and a great soldier, his greatness was too complex and vast for Shakespeare to be able to portray it successfully within the space of a single play, even had he so desired.

Although there is adequate justification for the play to be entitled *Julius Caesar*, Brutus appears to have the better claim to the principal tragic part, since it is he, and not Caesar, who is cast by the playwright in the heroic role.

Question 9.

Discuss the meaning of the tragic flaw in the Shakespearean hero with references to its occurrence in *Julius Caesar*.

Answer

Although he possesses many virtues, Brutus becomes a figure in tragedy because of the tragic flaw in this fine character. The tragic flaw is not any easily identifiable "bad quality." On the contrary, it would be hard to find an evil, dishonest or distasteful quality in the man. The tragic flaw in Brutus is that there is a subtle, but pervasive, drawback in almost every one of his admirable qualities. For instance, he is an idealist, but he is an unrealistic idealist. Therefore his idealism, put to the test, is no match for ruthlessness, cynicism and deceit. Brutus has a conscience, but it is a guilty conscience. He enters a cause against all his reasoning. He lets himself be flattered into joining the conspiracy, urged on by a concept of ancestral honor. He spends endless days and nights convincing himself against his better nature, for his theory of Julius Caesar is at war with his personal attitude toward Caesar. His devotion to the abstract virtues that he lives by removes him from the world of common men, and he is, consequently, so poor a judge of men's character that he brings about his own disaster. Firmly decisive on the point that none but Caesar shall die, the flaw in Brutus will not let him compromise his principles to the extent of protecting the action, the assassination, already taken. His refusal to eliminate Antony leads to his disaster and the downfall of his cause. Finally, his own conscience saw the killing of Caesar as murder, necessary, even glorious in terms of the state, but murder, nonetheless. His own conscience decided that, although the cause for which he killed was a noble one, the price had to be paid, even if it be his life. It is his guilty conscience that allows the spirit of Caesar to enter Brutus' subconscious and then his conscious being to bring about his defeat. In other words, Brutus has, in every virtue, a subtle consequence of harm to him, and this is the tragic flaw that, through his actions, his interactions, his emotions and his intellectual processes, brings him to his end. Yet, his death itself is not the tragedy. The tragic flaw has brought about the waste of all the virtues, the love and the life values of Brutus.

Question 10

Write a summary of the character of Caesar.

Answer

Shakespeare does not do justice, in this play, to the character of Caesar, perhaps the greatest man of the ancient world. Caesar is portrayed as an affected tyrant, pompous, superstitious and seeking a degree of determination and courage that he obviously lacks. Although the character of the dictator is seen to possess a certain majesty, it is a majesty that has deteriorated. His energy has become calmed by age, and the absolute power that he commands has corrupted the nobility of his character. His pride and boastfulness, his arrogance and pompousness all serve to make the audience dislike Caesar and, by comparison, to sympathize more with the conspirators in their plot to get rid of him. Once he is dead, however, his true greatness is revealed. In death, he is shown as mightier than in life, and, gradually, one warms to his memory, while viewing the motives of his murderers with increasing suspicion and distaste.

Question 11.
Contrast and compare the differing views held by Brutus and Cassius of the character of Julius Caesar.

Answer
Brutus likes and respects Julius Caesar. He is afraid, however, that if Caesar receives a crown, he may abuse his powers. Brutus believes, therefore, that the best interests of the people require that Caesar be prevented from becoming king.

Cassius dislikes and distrusts Caesar. He considers him unworthy, on personal grounds, of his respect. Moreover, he shares Brutus' view that, if the best interests of the people are to be considered, Caesar should not be crowned.

Question 12.
Is Caesar a superstitious man?

Answer
Caesar is probably no more superstitious than most educated Romans of his time. He is not overly concerned by what his wife, Calphurnia, tells him of her dreams. Although he sends a servant to consult the priests, he seems to ignore the subsequent message that the omens are unfavorable. When he eventually agrees not to go to the senate, it is not because of his own superstitious fears, but because he respects the pleadings of his wife, who appears almost hysterical. It requires little persuasion from Decius to cause Caesar to disregard his wife's fears and to change his mind for the last time. On his way to the senate house, he displays no evidence of concern, even mocking the soothsayer and ignoring his fateful reply. Finally, he makes no great effort to read the petition presented by Artemidorus, the scanning of which would have put him on guard and, perhaps, saved his life.

Question 13.
Briefly outline the character of Cassius.

Answer

The character of Cassius is contrasted with that of Brutus. Cassius is by far the better conspirator, but the worse man. His motives for plotting the assassination of Caesar, while mixed, are the result of his experience of men and affairs. Unlike Brutus, he is not concerned with what might be, but with what is. Cassius believes that, having entered the plot, the conspirators should not jeopardize its ultimate success by scruples. It is to Cassius' credit that his tolerance of Brutus prevents the breaking up of the partnership, but this accommodation of Brutus proves their undoing.

Cassius' shrewd appraisal of other men is evident when he appeals to Brutus' love of freedom and, again, when he plays upon the superstitious fears of Casca. Compared with Brutus, he seems harsh and unattractive. However, although he is frequently irritable, he can be tactful on occasion and he possesses a strong sense of personal loyalty, which Brutus lacks. Perhaps the most endearing thing about Cassius is his liking and respect for Brutus. Evidently, Cassius is somewhat awed by the moral superiority of his friend. This feeling serves to restrain him, to put his baser motives to shame and, involuntarily, to bring out the best in him.

Question 14.

Describe the main character traits of Marc Antony.

Answer

Marc Antony's part in *Julius Caesar* is that of an angry, yet attractive, young man, a powerful speaker and a bold, quick-witted schemer. He departs from his habitual shrewdness of character in that he appears, unlike Caesar, to be unsuspicious of Cassius, while he is entirely unaware of the assassination plot. His shrewdness becomes evident, however, in the confusion immediately after the murder. Escaping to Caesar's house, he takes possession of the dead man's papers and then confronts the assassins, risking all on his estimate of the character of Brutus. With great cunning, he flatters Brutus into giving him permission to speak, during the funeral ceremonies, as "Caesar's friend." His subsequent speech reveals his extraordinary manipulative powers and his keen insight into the character of the mob. His personality is in marked contrast to that of Brutus, while he has something in common with Cassius.

Unlike Brutus, he is not hampered by moral scruples. His many faults—cruelty, treachery, coldness and dishonesty—are obvious. On the other hand, there is much about him to admire, particularly his deep affection for Caesar and his determination to bring about the downfall of the conspirators. It is this spirit of devotion and loyalty toward Caesar that serves to ennoble Antony's character, since one feels that a man who can appreciate greatness in another has a touch of the same quality himself. There is little evidence in *Julius Caesar* of the military genius that made Marc Antony his master's most outstanding general, and there are only vague and casual references to the self-indulgence that eventually led to his downfall.

Question 15.

Compare the personalities of Cassius and Brutus.

Answer

It appears that Shakespeare designed the character of Cassius as a foil to that of Brutus. Cassius is essentially a man of the world and he understands his fellow men much better than Brutus may ever hope to do, since the latter is an idealist. Of the two, the character of Cassius is more readily understandable than that of Brutus. Having associated freely with other men, Cassius has learned to weigh their motives and he seems fully aware of his own. He despises Julius Caesar and he is perfectly willing to enter the plot for that reason alone. Cassius is entirely content to let Brutus seek a more philosophical motive. Thus, Cassius says of his friend:

> Well, Brutus, thou art noble; yet, I see,
> That honourable metal may be wrought
> From that it is dispos'd......
>
> (Act I, Scene 2)

While Cassius is no philosopher, he appears to appreciate the limitations of philosophy more shrewdly than Brutus does.

Frequently, Cassius reveals a quick temper, while he shows a sense of burning hatred for both Caesar and Marc Antony. Brutus also has a temper, but his anger tends to be short-lived. Brutus says of his hot-tempered friend:

O Cassius, you are yoked with a lamb
That carries anger as the flint bears fire

(Act IV, Scene 3)

Cassius' motives for killing Caesar are questionable, yet he is better qualified to lead the conspiracy than Brutus is. In every matter in which the two men differ, events prove Cassius to be the better judge. Marc Antony clearly should have been killed with Julius Caesar. But Brutus is allowed to have his way in this matter. Marc Antony should also never have been allowed to speak at the funeral ceremonies. Later, Brutus' decision to march on Philippi and attack the enemy at that point is a tactical error. The same lack of military skill and judgment is revealed by the haste with which Brutus leads his troops against Octavius Caesar and, in so doing, loses contact with Cassius.

There is little that is petty in the character of Cassius, and it is difficult to despise him totally. He may be blamed, perhaps, for involving a man like Brutus in the assassination plot. It may be that, while fully aware of the dangers of such a step, he overestimated his ability to curb and control his more cautious, but headstrong colleague.

It has been said of Brutus, that "he pays humanity the compliment of being rational." His many blunders and errors of judgment result from the fact that he makes few allowances for the overwhelming power of human emotions. He is inaccurate in his estimation of men and affairs. A self-righteous man, he fails to appreciate that others are not as virtuous as he.

Question 16.
Write a brief character sketch of Calphurnia.

Answer
Calphurnia adds to and reflects the character of Caesar, in the same way that Portia serves to reveal certain aspects of the character of Brutus. Calphurnia is a harsher type of woman than Portia and she appears to be somewhat domineering. Despite her urgent and hysterical fears for Caesar concerning his intended visit to the senate house, Calphurnia fails to win her point. Caesar is only half convinced by her urgent pleadings and he listens readily to the persistent Decius Brutus. However, one may not justly blame Calphurnia for her lack of persuasive powers, since her husband is torn by conflicting emotions—his

professed contempt for the priests, his fear of being thought a coward and his concern that this might be the last chance for him to receive the crown. Calphurnia reveals herself as superstitious and excitable. In her concern for Caesar's safety, she is not above telling a lie, if such a course will ensure the safety of her husband.

Question 17.
Write a brief character sketch of Casca.

Answer
Casca is first encountered in Act I, Scene 2, when he is heard calling loudly for silence as Caesar begins to speak. Later, however, he tells Brutus and Cassius what took place when Caesar was offered a crown, and of his refusal of it. His manner in talking to the others is bluntly ironical and appears to lend support to Cassius' insistence that, in his youth, he was "quick metal." Yet Casca is clearly shown to be superstitious by his actions and attitude during the night of the storm, and it is in these circumstances that he is easily persuaded by Cassius to join the conspiracy. Later, at Brutus' house, it is evident that Casca is somewhat reluctant to assert himself and that he leans rather heavily upon the opinions of others. It is not clear why Casca strikes the first blow at Caesar's assassination. Likewise, it is uncertain why he strikes Caesar from behind and why his blow is ineffective. Yet it would seem unfair to Casca to dismiss him as a mere coward. Like his fellow conspirators, he will risk all for success, and it is with an air of fierce determination that he gives the prearranged signal for Caesar's murder, despite his inept use of the assassin's dagger.

Question 18.
Write a character sketch of Octavius.

Answer
Octavius, the nephew and adopted son of Julius Caesar, is shown as a man of action who has a sense of burning revenge against the conspirators. The qualities that will make the future Caesar are hinted at during the course of the play. Octavius is a man of few words. Despite his youth, he clearly demonstrates his independence of Antony. He is not convinced by the latter's criticism of Lepidus, nor will he allow Antony to dominate him,

even in military matters. During the parley with the enemy commanders before the Battle of Philippi, he shows his impatience of "words before blows" and cuts short the argument by a challenge to action. In his final speech in the play, he demonstrates that he is in charge of affairs.

Question 19.
Briefly describe the character of Portia.

Answer
Portia may be described as the counterpart of Brutus. In the same way that Brutus is proudly aware of his illustrious family heritage, so is Portia conscious of being "so fathered and so husbanded." Like Brutus, she has an extremely sensitive nature, although her ancestry and her relationship to Brutus instil in her some measure of self-control. She is a practical and affectionate lady, seeking to share her husband's worries and anxieties. Her distress at Brutus' silence indicates that he had previously considered her worthy of his confidence. She shows herself as determined to share the secret that appears to have divided her from Brutus. She is motivated not by idle curiosity but by a genuine desire to help him. As proof of her strength and to comfort and support her husband, she gashes herself and suffers the pain without complaint. However, on the morning of the assassination, her composure gives way under the stress of great emotion, and she almost betrays the secret so well kept by others. Nevertheless, Portia manages to control herself sufficiently to invent an excuse for her incautious remark, and she removes Lucius' suspicions by sending the boy on a needless errand. After the murder, she finds it impossible to endure the strain of waiting for the outcome of the conspiracy. Gradually, her mind becomes so affected that, with the determination of madness, she "swallows fire."

Question 20.
Write a general description of the Roman mob.

Answer
On the whole, the citizens of Rome are presented by Shakespeare in an unfavorable light. While sometimes interesting as individuals, the citizens, regarded as a mob, are shown to be changeable, unreasoning, treacherous and savage. In the open-

ing scene of the play, the cobbler displays a sense of humor when talking rather freely and scornfully with the tribunes. The same man later shows good sense during Brutus' funeral speech but he is very active in the subsequent questioning of Cinna, the poet.

Yet it appears from the remarks of the tribunes at the beginning of the play that the Roman citizens are fickle and subject to significant shifts of loyalty. Casca expresses the same view when, speaking of the "wenches" who had sympathized with Caesar, he says that they would have done the same if he had stabbed their mothers. Thus, when urged to remember the former glories of Pompey, they are silent; yet, when asked to look at the mutilated corpse of Caesar, they are violent and ferocious.

When Brutus speaks to them in measured, balanced prose, they appreciate the reasonableness of his address. When Antony deliberately plays on their feelings and finally weeps, they spontaneously follow his lead.

Their conflicting cries demonstrate their inability to retain more than one idea at a time. Their need of firm leadership is indicated by their gullibility and their frequent shifts and changes of opinion.

Their importance in the play is threefold: The mob is an obvious force in deciding the outcome of the conspiracy; they serve as the visible counterpart of the invisible forces of the supernatural; they act as a sounding board for the effectiveness of the principal speakers and provide the realistic, living background to the main characters and incidents of the drama.

Question 21.
Compare the deaths of Cassius and Brutus.

Answer
Cassius, when mistakenly convinced that all is lost, reminds his servant, Pindarus, of the conditions under which the latter's life was spared: Pindarus promised unquestioning obedience to his master's will. Cassius then orders Pindarus to hold his sword, so that he can fall on it. Pindarus obeys without question, although perhaps with reluctance.

When Brutus finally decides that there is no alternative to suicide, he is with four of his followers—Clitus, Dardanius, Volumnius and Strato. He asks the first three, in turn, to hold his sword, but they refuse because of their affection for him. When Brutus is left alone with Strato, the latter is persuaded, although with great reluctance, to perform the task that the other three declined.

In general, it should be noted that the contrast lies in the manner in which each asks his servant to kill him. While Cassius is harsh and abrupt, Brutus displays both mildness and consideration.

Question 22.

Since Calphurnia and Portia contribute little to the action of the play, justify the fact that they appear at all.

Answer

By their agitation and concern for the well-being of their respective husbands, they serve to heighten the feeling of suspense felt by the audience. Portia's successful pleading to be her husband's confidante serves to demonstrate the essential kindness and considerateness of Brutus' nature. Calphurnia's unsuccessful pleading to restrain her husband from attending the senate house serves to reveal something of Caesar's indecisive nature and his pompousness.

Question 23.

Contrast and compare the relationship between Caesar and Calphurnia with that of Brutus and Portia.

Answer

Although Caesar appears to love Calphurnia he does not display much respect for her intellect. He seems to regard her as an impulsive child—someone to be humored, but hardly to be trusted with weighty matters of state. Although Calphurnia speaks sternly to Caesar about his attending the senate house, one has the impression that her husband's temporary agreement results from his desire to avoid further nagging, rather than from any trust in her native intuition or her shrewd appraisal of political matters. Portia is easily overshadowed by the astute Decius Brutus, whose ''logical'' explanation of her troubled dreams finally convinces Caesar and reduces her to a helpless and uneasy silence.

By contrast, the relationship between Brutus and Portia is one of tender love and complete understanding. Brutus conceals the assassination plot from Portia because of his desire not to burden her with his troubles. There cannot be secrets between them for long, however. When Portia demands to share her husband's burdens, Brutus must give in to her request, since she convinces him of her powers of endurance. He was apparently never in doubt as to her intellectual qualities. There appears to be complete harmony of mind between Brutus and Portia, and each continues to worry about the other. Immediately before the murder, Portia is shown to be frantic with anxiety. She later "swallows fire" when it appears that the military campaign may not be successful. Brutus is overcome when he hears of his wife's death. Indeed, it is this news that partly accounts for his bitter quarrel with Cassius, in which he shows himself to be both emotional and inconsistent.

Question 24.

List the principal mistakes made by Brutus after he has become the leader of the conspiracy.

Answer

a. He refuses to permit an oath of secrecy. Presumably Artemidorus hears of the plot from one of the conspirators.

b. He refuses to allow Cicero to join the conspiracy. A brilliant and popular orator with great influence, Cicero might have been able to offset the effects of Marc Antony's provocative speech.

c. He refuses to allow Antony to be assassinated when Caesar is. Antony's actions do most to bring about the downfall of the conspirators.

d. He not only permits Marc Antony to speak at Caesar's funeral, but makes the grave error of allowing him to have the last word, which sets in motion a popular rebellion.

e. At Sardis, Brutus speaks bitterly of Cassius in the presence of inferiors. Not only is this a serious breach of etiquette, but it would do nothing, if repeated, to improve the morale of the troops.

f. The reasons for the quarrel at Sardis are the supposed wrongs of Cassius. Brutus fails to see, as Cassius points out, that extraordinary situations require extraordinary measures. Moreover, Brutus displays inconsistency, since he not only blames his friend for raising money improperly, but scolds Cassius for denying him some part of it.

g. In spite of his lack of military experience, Brutus over-rules Cassius, the more experienced commander. Brutus insists on marching from Sardis to Philippi and meeting the enemy there. This action goes against the advice of Cassius and proves to be a fatal error.

Question 25.

Summarize Marc Antony's speech to the citizens during Caesar's funeral ceremonies, distinguishing the stages by which he excites them.

Answer

Marc Antony's speech may be divided into four stages.

a. At the beginning of the speech, the mob is hostile, as is shown by the fourth citizen, who says: "'Twere best he speak no harm of Brutus here." Realizing this, Marc Antony begins calmly and reasonably, following Brutus' instructions. He restates the latter's argument, with the intention of later destroying it. By mentioning Caesar's military triumphs and the consequent improvement of the state's finances, his concern for the poor, and his repeated rejection of the crown, Marc Antony (despite his repeated protests) virtually disproves Brutus' charge that the dead man was ambitious. Knowing well how powerful emotion can prove, he puts reason aside and soon reaches the point where he pretends to be overcome with grief, pausing to measure the effect of his introductory words. By now, the mob is attentive and largely sympathetic, and this feeling is made clear by one citizens, who remarks: "Methinks there is much reason in his sayings."

b. When Marc Antony continues, he speaks about the pathos of Caesar's assassination. A great man has fallen and is being shown little respect, he says. He hints at what might happen should he attempt to stir them to mutiny; this he will not do, since he would prefer to wrong anybody but the "honourable" assassins of Caesar. By now, Marc Antony has become ironical and he uses the word "honourable" nine times in reference to Brutus and the others. He then suddenly produces Caesar's will, hinting at rich bequests, in vague terms designed to excite the curiosity of his audience.

c. Realizing that the citizens are now on his side, Marc Antony makes the most of the speech-maker's trick of suspense. Pretending to be reluctant, but reinforced by the words of two of the crowd, he descends from his platform and joins them. But instead of continuing to talk about the will, he proceeds to play upon their pity for the fallen hero. He craftily refers to Caesar's defeat of the Nervii and then points out the various holes in the dead man's robe, identifying each one with an individual assassin, speaking at some length about the treachery of Brutus. By now, since he believes that the mob has been completely won over, Marc Antony makes no further pretence to speak within the terms of his promise made to the conspirators. While claiming to lack all powers of oratory, he hints that the sight of Caesar's mutilated corpse might be sufficient to "move the stones of Rome to rise and mutiny."

d. By this time, the citizens are in a state of angry excitement. Before their anger decreases, however, Marc Antony reminds them that they have not yet heard the terms of Caesar's will. He then reads just enough of the will to suit his purpose, which is to impress upon the people that they were the objects of Caesar's special love and concern. By doing so, he sets the mob in motion. The people rush away, mad for revenge, and the conspirators are in grave danger.

Question 26.

Discuss the manner in which dramatic suspense is maintained in the play up to the end of Act III.

Answer

It is the climax of the play—the assassination of Caesar—that an audience would naturally anticipate, and, accordingly, Shakespeare achieved the maximum dramatic effect by approaching the murder plot in a gradual manner.

He does not simply mention Cassius, Casca, Cinna and Calphurnia. Instead, all these characters are made to show alarm or concern at the strange events associated with the storm. The murder of Caesar, then, is gradually approached through the event of a fantastic natural phenomenon that holds, and even strains, one's attention. Moreover, it is noteworthy how carefully Shakespeare draws the attention of his audience to the gradual passage of time before the murder. Thus, one's attention is successively drawn to the fact that it is night, dawn, eight o'clock and nine o'clock.

From the point when Cassius begins to persuade Brutus to enter the plot, the action of the play tends to speed up, and the audience eagerly anticipates the actual murder scene. One shares with Brutus his growing concern, when he says:

Between the acting of a dreadful thing
And the first motion, all the interim is
Like a phantasma or a hideous dream.
(Act II, Scene 1)

There is the stark and graphic scene in which Brutus eventually meets the other conspirators in his orchard, to be followed by the appearance of the pathetically anxious Portia. The subsequent action is drawn out by the scene at Caesar's house, where the distracted Calphurnia is attempting to convince her husband to remain at home, the sly and persuasive Decius Brutus appears and, eventually, the rest of the senators arrive. The period between the departure of Caesar and his followers and their arrival at the senate house is enlivened by the attempt of Artemidorus to warn Caesar, Portia's evident anxiety when talking to Lucius, and the second appearance of the soothsayer.

Shortly after the beginning of Act III, Scene 1, Caesar is assassinated. From this point on, the action of the play tends to slow down. Yet this fact is not immediately obvious. The rest of Act III is devoted to the commotion and excitement in Rome; the magnificent and moving Forum scene, in which Brutus and Marc Antony address the people; the shift of public sentiment to the support of Antony; and the savage temper of the mob, as demonstrated by the final scene in Act III, in which Cinna, the poet, is murdered.

Question 27.

"The play tends to drag after the third act." Discuss this statement, and show how the playwright retains the interest of his audience.

Answer

Audiences have probably felt that the play tends to drag after the murder in Act III, Scene 1. However, this fact is not immediately apparent, since Shakespeare is able to retain the interest of his audience by general excitement, the funeral ceremonies in the Forum and the murder of Cinna, the poet, by the enraged mob.

The subsequent meeting of the triumvirs, Antony, Octavius and Lepidus, is relatively uninteresting, since its emotional level and therefore, its dramatic appeal is much lower than what has gone before. This is so, despite the fact that Shakespeare permits no pause between the high point of Brutus' fortunes and the point at which the forces leading to his destruction are set in motion.

The audience has barely witnessed Caesar's death before it is led to anticipate the ultimate defeat of the conspirators and to take the liveliest interest in the rising fortunes of Marc Antony and Octavius Caesar. Shakespeare skilfully adds to the dramatic effect in various ways. While Brutus' death is inevitable, it comes about slowly, during a period of drawn-out suspense. Thus, the audience learns of trouble between the two leaders, before they are seen face to face, when Brutus says to Lucilius of Cassius:

> Thou hast describ'd
> A hot friend cooling.
>
> (Act IV, Scene 3)

When the quarrel is finally settled and the scene has fallen into silence and darkness, Caesar's ghost appears and warns that the settlement of the leaders' differences is unlikely to ensure success in the forthcoming battle.

In Act V, Scene 1, there is a brief truce between the opposing factions. Despite the bitter remarks of the rival commanders, one may tend to consider, the possibility of some permanent compromise. In the same scene, Cassius talks gloomily to Messala of the numerous omens observed during the march from Sardis to Philippi. The suspense is increased by Brutus and Cassius when they say farewell to each other on the assumption that the battle may be lost and that they may never meet again.

The last three scenes are believably, but not excessively, drawn out. Brutus seems at first to be temporarily on the rise, but Cassius makes an entirely unforeseeable blunder and commits suicide. Brutus refuses to be captured and executed and he is probably saved from this fate by Lucilius' impersonation of him. Finally, in Brutus' suicide, his nobility of character is stressed by the reluctance of his friends and followers to be responsible for his death. All these incidents, interesting as they undoubtedly are, have to do with the lengthening of the play far beyond its natural climax. Only gradually does the wheel of fortune come to a halt.

Question 28.

How does Shakespeare use darkness to intensify his dramatic effects in *Julius Caesar*?

Answer

In Act I, Scene 3, we are introduced at once, by the dialogue between Casca and Cicero, into a scene of profound disquiet. A storm of unparalleled intensity hangs over Rome. The darkness of the night is intensified and enlivened by the rumbling of thunder and the flashing of lightning. Casca, in contrast to the calm Cicero, is apparently cringing, as though he expects to be killed at any moment. His sword is drawn, as though to fight off the horrors of which he speaks at some length. Thus, the character of the frightened and gullible Casca is contrasted with that of the matter-of-fact and unemotional Cicero and the crafty Cassius. We are left in no doubt that it is night and that a storm is raging, in spite of the apparent naturalness of the conversation. The darkness of the night seems to echo the sinister plot that is unfolding, while the constant physical reminders of the storm serve to suggest the apparent violence of the natural elements.

By the beginning of Act II, Scene 1, in Brutus' orchard, the storm has died down somewhat; both thunder and lightning may be imagined to be less frequent and more remote. The fact that it is night is, however, made apparent by Brutus' opening remarks to Lucius, his servant. But the former's complaint about the darkness of the night may be taken also to reflect his state of indecision as to whether he will participate in the conspiracy. By frequent references, we are shown how the night progresses toward dawn, while simultaneously Brutus decides to become a party to the plot, to assume its leadership, to arrange its details and to confide in Portia, his wife. The grey lines that streak the morning clouds are apparently indicative of the coming day, which is to be disturbed in more senses than one. The correspondence between the turbulence and darkness of the night to the evil schemes of the assassins is made apparent by Brutus just before he is joined by Cassius and the rest. He declares:

> They are the faction. O conspiracy!
> Sham'st thou to show thy dangerous brow by night,
> When evils are most free?

In Act IV, Scene 3, the audience is transferred to Brutus' camp near Sardis, where the two leaders argue bitterly. We become aware of the approach of darkness during the reconciliation scene, when Brutus issues orders to his commanders to settle the troops for the night. In a hushed atmosphere and against a background of deepening darkness, Brutus reveals to Cassius the fact and the manner of Portia's death. Candles are then brought, as Messala and Titinius join the others, and the plan of battle is discussed. Lucius brings Brutus' gown, and Cassius and the rest depart. There follow indications of drowsiness and talk of sleep. Lucius, at Brutus' request, plays for a minute or two on his instrument but soon falls asleep. Not wishing to disturb the boy, Brutus attempts to read as the darkness deepens. The utter silence becomes apparent. At this point, a moment of great intensity, Caesar's ghost appears. The calm manner of Brutus' conversation with his "evil genius" does little to break the spell. But after the disappearance of the ghost, Brutus becomes more concerned. He calls out loudly to all about him. There are anxious questions and confused answers. For a few moments, as the scene closes, there is some bustle and activity. The spell of silence and darkness has been effectively broken. The drama of battle is nearer.

Question 29.

What relationship does the ritual "blood bath" have to the theme of the play?

Answer

The bathing of the conspirators' hands and forearms in the blood of Caesar was neither a Roman nor an Elizabethan custom. This gesture was Shakespeare's device for displaying vividly, in action and situation, the idea that Brutus wanted to impress upon the people of Rome: once having decided on assassination (in itself a despicable crime), Brutus had to justify the means by raising these to the level of a ritual sacrifice.

Of course, the purpose of this ritual ceremony seems inconsistent when we remember that Brutus has prefaced this ritual gesture with the cynical remark that, by granting Caesar death, the conspirators are his friends in having "abridg'd his time of fearing death," and that Brutus has refused to "hack the limbs" (kill Antony) on the grounds that the conspirators are "sacrificers, but not butchers." But then, this is part of the subtle irony that Shakespeare combines with his characterization: Brutus' virtue is a convenient pretence for his stubborn will and the belief in his own infallibility.

The symbolism of the blood ritual is twofold: if the murder of Caesar is indeed senseless, then the conspirators are "up to their elbows in blood." If the assassination is justified, then the bloody murder is really an act of deliverance that will bring new strength to Rome. Brutus, trying to justify by reason an unjustifiable deed, cannot see the supreme irony: this bloodletting is symbolic of the blood that will be spilled in a disordered Rome.

Question 30.

To what extent does the element of irony enter into the characterizations of Brutus, Caesar, Cassius and Antony?

Answer

The play is filled with ironic situations, but these are the ironies of fate: Brutus dismisses the wise advice of Cassius, particularly in the case of Antony; Cassius commits suicide after he mistakes Brutus' initial victory for defeat; Caesar, who has always used people for his own ends, cannot recognize friend from enemy.

Nevertheless, the subtlest form of irony lies in the characterizations of the four leading protagonists. There is no clear distinction between white and black, good and evil. The virtuous Brutus is willfully blind to his own defects: he despises tyranny but he must lead. He hates treachery and deceit but rationalizes the murder of a trusting friend, on unsupported charges, in the interests of morality. He condemns questionable practices but nags Cassius for not sharing the "collections" with which the honorable Brutus will not soil his hands. In saving Rome from a benevolent tyrant, he plunges it into civil strife and bloodshed, yet he remains convinced to the end that his deeds will be justified. Forgetting that he has deceived Caesar and that Antony has deceived him, Brutus blindly claims that he has never met a friend who was untrue to him.

Caesar, who boasts of constancy equal to that of the North Star, can be swayed by the flattery of the false Decius. Antony and Octavius, who had been bitterly insulting their enemies, show respect for them when referring to them as the "last of the noble Romans" and "the noblest Roman of them all." Perhaps the most ironic twist of character is evident in Antony and Cassius: both are opportunistic realists, completely without scruples, yet each is affected by the softest of human emotions, a pure love for friends who show little feeling for them.

NOTES

NOTES

NOTES

NOTES

NOTES

NOTES